MITCHELL BEAZLEY

COOK YOUR OWN
VEG

CAROL KLEIN

Cook Your Own Veg
by Carol Klein

First published in Great Britain in 2008 by Mitchell Beazley,
an imprint of Octopus Publishing Group Limited,
2–4 Heron Quays, London E14 4JP.
An Hachette Livre UK Company

© Octopus Publishing Group Limited 2008
Text © Carol Klein 2008
Photographs © Howard Sooley 2008

A CIP catalogue record for this book is available from the
British Library.

ISBN 978-1-84533-407-9

While all reasonable care has been taken during the preparation
of this edition, neither the publisher, editors, nor the authors
can accept responsibility for any consequences arising from
the use thereof or from the information contained therein.

Commissioning Editor: Becca Spry
Art Director: Tim Foster
Deputy Art Director: Yasia Williams-Leedham
Designer: Miranda Harvey
Project Editor: Ruth Patrick
Editor: Susan Fleming
Photographer: Howard Sooley
Words: Carol and Neil Klein
Styling: Isobel de Cordova and Helen Trent
Home Economist: Sara Lewis
Production Manager: Lucy Carter
Index: Helen Snaith

Typeset in PMN Caecilia
Colour reproduction by Sang Choy, Singapore
Printed and bound by Toppan, China

contents

introduction

Imagine the most delicious vegetables you have ever eaten. A simple salad, green leaves picked fresh and tender on a fine summer morning with the dew still glistening on them, a mêlée of tastes and textures, melded together with the lightest of dressings. Or on a cold winter's night taking out of the Aga a dish of steaming, fragrant squash, its orange flesh soft and yielding under a crust of pine nuts and Parmesan. We have always loved cooking and eating vegetables, but when we first started growing our own at Glebe Cottage 30 years ago, we were struck by the difference in taste. Nothing has changed, every time the experience is new and exciting – a delight.

Taste is the over-riding consideration, but there are many other benefits. First and foremost everything is fresh, picked or lifted as it is needed in the kitchen, in just the right amounts. We grow organically; no chemicals are used anywhere in our garden, and we know exactly what is on and in our vegetables. The soil is enriched with home-made compost and leaf mould. Crops are mixed to keep down pests, and we use companion planting to confuse marauding invaders.

We can grow the varieties we like, the beans with the best flavour that are succulent without being stringy, the beetroot with the richest purple leaves or that have the best roots for eating raw or those that store best for an earthy winter treat. We can choose varieties that suit our soil and our geographical region. At one time gardeners would have concentrated on local vegetables that would have traditionally been grown in that area, but nowadays the choice of varieties offered commercially is circumscribed by the EU. Seed swapping is the answer to this prescription and the trend to maintain heritage varieties is resulting in a wider choice for those interested in growing, cooking and eating. When veg production is mechanized, growers need everything to ripen at the same time, machinery must be able to harvest efficiently and supermarkets demand uniform crops delivered on the agreed date. Taste and individuality go out of the window.

In the kitchen we need a steady supply of seasonal produce if possible for the whole year.

We need versatile vegetables that can be picked at different stages and be used in a variety of ways. If we select varieties carefully, the same carrot that could be pulled tender and young in midsummer could perhaps assume a different persona if left in the ground until the winter, then harvested as an ingredient for a hearty, warming soup. French beans picked young and cooked fleetingly for a delicacy on their own; or left a week longer to enliven a salad or summer combo; or left till the beans inside swell large enough to be evicted from the pod, but still fresh and green; or left for an Indian summer to dry them all bleached and hard in their, by now, papery pods.

The other thing you notice with vegetables you have grown yourself is their texture. Crisp and tender at the same time, they have a vitality and a squeaky resilience that you can't buy. If you happen to leave your vegetables lying around for a while you will be shocked at how limp and badly wilted they will have become. They will compare badly with the armies of regimented supermarket produce. Then you realize how commercial varieties have been selected and bred precisely for their long-lasting qualities. Their deterioration has to be slowed right down for a fortnight or more: they are bought on sight, on their appearance – no one tastes them first before buying – so above all else they have to look forever new.

Although you can pick your own veg at their exact peak of perfection, you are not cropping commercially, ruthlessly selecting for unblemished uniformity. Your organic veg will not have been sprayed with insecticide to prevent all insect attention and force-fed fertilizers to speed up uniform growth. You can tolerate bent beans, mysterious holes, curled leaves, forked roots, little and large, because they will all taste fine and anyway, you grew them yourself. Unless you have a catastrophic plague of locusts, you will have plenty of vegetables to share with your insect neighbours. Good cultivation and simple physical barriers such as fine netting will keep their attentions from getting out of hand. By gardening organically and by encouraging a wide range of wildlife through providing food and shelter, you will eventually establish a balance in your garden that will prevent either prey or predators from over-running the place.

My family and I gave up eating meat and poultry a long time ago, in distaste at the cruelty that industrially farmed animals have to endure. There are no pangs of conscience in loving the vegetables you grow, even though you know you will eventually end up eating them. They do however deserve an unjaded palate, and they may yet seduce you away from the salty, sugary, fatty, cranked-up food that comes out of a factory instead of your own kitchen, if they haven't done so already.

Finally, people are also recognizing that the Western wheat-meat-dairy diet is intrinsically unhealthy and unsustainable for the planet. You can feed ten vegetarians for the same resources and consequences it takes to feed one wheat-meat-dairy eater.

As to diets, the vegetable content of your diet will increase if you have grown your own, because it will all be irresistible. Regularly eating a wide range of different vegetables will cover almost all of your vitamin, mineral and fibre requirements. It is also a good idea to alternate the styles of recipes – raw, cooked in water, cooked in oil, cooked with dairy.

Fresh, raw vegetables contain all the available nutrients that are otherwise lost at high-temperatures, long cooking and storage, even refrigeration. Blanched and steamed are next best nutritionally, trading off the loss of nutrients against the easier digestibility that light cooking ensures. The modern taste for crisp, young vegetables means

that there is no call for boiled-to-death cooking.

Oil is the next cooking medium, and your delectable little produce deserves the best you can find. We favour olive oil and organic cold-pressed extra virgin olive oil is the purest; some people think it is too expensive to cook with and is sometimes fiery in flavour and has a low burning point (you can't get it very hot). Because we don't go for deep-frying, this has never been a problem for us as we only use it sparingly, adding water to a sautéed, stewed or sweated dish if required to prevent any burning.

Butter is still the only choice for some dishes and unsalted butter (with salt added to the recipe later) will cook better than the salty yellow stuff.

And as for cream, while it might have seemed a justifiable indulgence 30 years ago to smother something in double cream, it now seems like cardiac overkill, however special the occasion.

harvesting

Harvesting, reaping the rewards of your labour, has to be the most satisfying aspect of growing vegetables. If you are to make the very best of all you grow, then you need to pick it or dig it up at the optimum time. Often that is decided by what you are going to do with it in the kitchen. How are you going to eat it? If it is peas do you want to pick them in their infancy to enjoy snappy, crunchy pods? Perhaps it's a dish of petits pois, cooked simply and very briefly with no other adornment than a chunk of butter and a mint leaf or two, their brilliant colour as green as spring itself. For best results they must be picked at exactly the moment the peas reach the side of the pod but just before they start to exert any pressure. Only one way to find out, pop them and see, if it is too early nothing is wasted. In some households, peas never even reach the table but are consumed in transit, en masse.

The taste of raw peas is considered a delicacy by some. I think they are powerful – after all, these are seeds and packed with all the potency to make new plants. I like peas cooked – but only just cooked.

To dry peas to store them to use in hearty winter soups, stews and tagines, they must dry on the vine, their skins becoming puckered and seared. At whatever stage you are picking peas or beans, hold the main stem tightly with finger and thumb above and below the pod and pull it gently downwards close to the stem with the other hand.

Choosing varieties for their eventual use in the kitchen is one of the many refinements of growing vegetables, and very much a question of trial and error. Some varieties excel at one particular stage of growth and it makes sense to take advantage of these tasty periods, even if the veg isn't fully matured. One year you might be really into barbecued leeks, so a very young crop of 'Swiss Giant Evita' in July might be perfect. Let the same leeks overwinter into March the following year and you might detest the giants they have grown into. If you want carrots all year you might delight in forcing some baby 'Amsterdam' for a bunch of baby fingers for eating raw in May. You will just as likely build up a late crop of 'Autumn King' for slow-cooked stews.

If you want to use pods, go for one of the sugar snaps. Peas are divided into two groups: wrinkled and round. As a general rule, round-seeded varieties – 'Hurst Green Shaft' is one of the best, tried and tested for generations – produce a bumper crop of elegant pods full of

The optimum time for picking your vegetables is often decided by what you are going to do with them. If you are growing peas, you could pick them in their infancy and enjoy crunchy peas, (left) or when the peas are about to burst out of the pod (right).

small, neat peas ideal to eat simmered for a couple of minutes or to cook and liquidize to make the most verdant soup ever. If you want to dry peas, try marrowfat varieties, the wrinkly ones that have more starch, which increases as they get riper.

The seeds of both peas and beans are packed with protein. Haricots and borlotti beans can be eaten as green beans, podded and eaten as fresh beans when big enough or left to dry, collected and stored. French beans must be eaten when they are young, for as soon as they start to mature, skins toughen and their succulence is lost.

Though they are good raw they taste even better steamed for one minute, or two at the most, eaten hot with butter or oil or left to go cold, dressed and consumed. Just like a dish of peas they need nothing else. Runner beans make more substantial fare. They are probably the most productive vegetable you can grow – and the trick is to pick them every day. Far better to store perfect pods in the fridge for a day than pick beans that are fresh but tough. Courgettes, too, grow and ripen so quickly, you have to seize them when they are the right size for your recipe. Asparagus may make you wait for a panful, but it's worth it.

Despite their various designations as being 'French' or 'Borlotti' or 'Haricots', all the aforementioned beans hail from the Americas, and only broad or fava beans come from

Trying to make sure I have collected all the courgettes of the best size. I will have to come back again tomorrow, as the fruits can quadruple in size overnight!

Europe, although they are grown now all over the world. This wonderful global vegetable intercourse runs parallel with that of the interaction of cuisines. We can learn so much from each other about how to grow and when to harvest vegetables as well as how to use them in the kitchen. French country cooking has inspired us to revere baby beans and tiny peas; Italy has shown us how to eat baby courgettes and even to stuff the flowers.

Salads and all green leaves, cauliflower, calabrese, broccoli and all the brassicas lose condition not to mention flavour and nutrients on the journey between plot and pot. When you grow your own, the journey is measured in feet rather than mega-miles.

Courgettes and summer squashes are best harvested frequently with the female flowers just beginning to fizzle, otherwise they will have become marrows before you

can say 'Cinderella'. In the case of pumpkins and winter squash however, when you are intending to store fruits for winter consumption, they should gather all the sun they can and be left to toughen up their outside skins, severing them from the plant in the short days of late autumn when leaves have started to shrivel.

Roots grow in the ground, and when that is the part of the plant we are planning to eat, that is the best place for them until they are needed. Young carrots, beetroot and new potatoes can be dug or pulled just before they are to be consumed. Main crop potatoes for winter storage are dug when foliage has died right back. Dig early on a dry day and leave on the surface of the soil, packing into thick paper bags or hessian sacks when dry.

Late carrots and beetroot are left to mature in the ground until the extremes of winter send them under cover in a port, outbuilding or clamp. Parsnips, cabbages, sprouts and leeks can all stand sentry outside and will taste all the better for a few frostings.

preparing the soil for next year

Dig some old muck into your designated plot in the autumn or winter before planting peas or beans, which love rich fare. They can be accompanied by spinach, onions, garlic or shallots.

The most important factor in determining the health, vigour and taste of veg is the soil in which they grow. Organic gardeners know that the soil sustains life, and the process by which nature recycles materials to feed the soil is part of an ongoing chain. It has worked for millions of years in nature and for thousands of years adopted by us in our gardens. Feeding the soil, encouraging soil-borne organisms to break it down and allowing plants to take what they need, is a balanced and sustainable practice.

Making compost is at the heart of the process. It does not matter how you make your compost as long as it works. Compost bins and tumblers, compost heaps and wormeries are all excellent ways to produce it. You can use any ingredients that have lived excluding cooked food, but try to achieve a balance of elements by incorporating layers of green waste with cardboard packaging to aerate the heap and, most importantly, physically turn the whole thing as often as you can.

Compost is such a precious commodity, there never seems to be enough of it. There are ways to supplement it though. One of the best is to use green manure. Whenever a patch of land stands fallow, even if it's only a few square feet

and only for a little time, it is worth sowing it with a green manure crop. This will prevent nutrient loss and erosion by rain, fix nitrogen in the soil in the case of leguminous crops and can be dug in before other crops are grown on it, thus boosting fertility.

Leaf mould is another excellent source of humus. If you have deciduous trees in or overhanging the garden, pile their leaves in a simple container: four wooden posts hammered into the soil with wire-mesh sides. And if you have no trees, the local council is often only too pleased to give leaves away as roads are cleared of debris in the autumn.

Try to rotate your crops. Each kind of crop has specific requirements and needs different amounts of nutrients and minerals from the soil. If groups of crops are rotated and planted in another piece of ground each year, the empty soil can be fed to give the next group of plants exactly what it needs. This well-proven practice also

A short breathing space at Glebe Cottage to take out the early spring crops before the summer ones take off.

helps cut down on soil-borne pests and diseases that cannot build up in the way they would if the same crops were continually grown in the same place.

If you have enough space, divide your growing area into four plots. If you are starting from scratch, designate plot 1 to legumes and dig in some old muck, ideally in the autumn or winter before planting, mixing it into the soil with a fork. Even if it is not dug in, it will eventually be incorporated by worms. The pea and bean family loves rich fare and will relish muck or any organic matter. They can be accompanied by leafy spinach and extra onions, garlic or shallots.

Use a general fertilizer, seaweed, 'fish, blood and bone' or a 'green manure' of sacrificial seedlings, in the other three plots. Plant roots in plot 2, brassicas in plot 3 and permanent crops in plot 4. The latter are crops that can stay in their plot every year. Rhubarb, artichokes (both globe and Jerusalem) and, if there is room, even asparagus could take up a long lease here. Potatoes and tomatoes can be fitted in wherever you have space, even in containers.

In the second year follow legumes in plot 1 with roots, bulbs and fruiting vegetables, including onions, leeks, carrots, parsnips, potatoes, squash and courgettes. This plot needs no muck but will benefit from an application of wood ash, if you're lucky enough to have it, and a general organic fertilizer. I rake this in in February or March.

In the third year for plot 1 more organic fertilizer and a dressing of garden lime will get the ground ready for brassicas, the huge and varied cabbage clan that also includes broccoli, cauliflowers, calabrese and turnips.

The roots that were in plot 2 in year one are followed in year two by brassicas, then legumes in year three. The brassicas that were in plot 3 in year one are followed in year two by legumes, then roots in year three. Just remember to follow legumes with roots.

three sisters planting

In regions of the world that have a continental climate (roasting hot in the summer and freezing cold in the winter), growing conditions are very different from those we experience in the UK. It is too chilly in prolonged cold spells to think of growing anything, so in the hot summers staple vegetables have to be grown in abundance, stored and put by for the austere months of winter.

The Native American Iroquois women grew the food and were the main providers of consistently available food. If hunting was good the men might bring home game but, especially in the winter, it was the three main staples – maize, beans and pumpkins – that could be relied upon even in the depths of the winter. All three yield a crop that can be stored dry and utilized long after it has finished growing. Beans could be taken from their pods and stored. Pumpkins, with their skin toughened and hard, would last almost indefinitely, and after their flesh was eaten, the skin was recycled and used for mats and roofing. Maize, what we now call sweetcorn, was stored as cobs or loose grain to be ground into flour until the time came to till the land again and eat fresh produce. Not only were these three crops valued for winter sustenance, but the seeds of all three could be kept and used to sow afresh the next spring.

Three sisters planting involves planting three different plants alongside each other. Each plant benefits from the others in the trilogy.

To make maximum use of the land they exploited a beautiful symbiosis between the three. A small mound would be made and into it planted a single seed of maize. One stride further on in each direction would be another mound and another seed. A few days later a single bean seed or perhaps two (the extra for insurance) would be pushed into the earth alongside the germinating sweetcorn. In the hollows created between the mounds, a pumpkin seed was sown, pressed into the warm earth. Any excess moisture drained into the hollow, giving the developing pumpkin plant the moisture needed to develop its large leaves and creeping vine-like stems along which, eventually, flowers and finally fruit would form. The leaves of the pumpkin helped the ground retain moisture while suppressing

When all danger of frost has passed, sturdy young sweetcorn and squash plants that have been started off in pots are brought to the three sisters bed.

The sweetcorn are spaced out and planted on a mound of soil, a French bean or two are pressed in close by, and squashes are planted in the dips.

weeds. The corn would offer a convenient support for the bean to climb and the bean, in common with all legumes, would benefit itself and its neighbours by helping provide extra nitrogen through the action of the nodules on its roots.

All three plants had something to offer to the relationship and benefited from it in return. The idea not only has its own poetry but it works. Choose a tall variety of sweetcorn,

a French or borlotti bean with reasonable manners and a squash or small pumpkin that will enjoy clambering around without trying to take over. Start all three in individual pots in April and plant out when frost is no longer a danger. Put the sweetcorn in first, 60cm (2ft) apart on a mound. Plant a French bean close by and put the squash or courgette in between in the hollow created by making the mounds. The three sisters will grow together in harmony.

spring

perennials

asparagus

One of the greatest benefits of growing and cooking your own is eating luxurious crops at exactly the right moment. Asparagus is at the pinnacle of the epicurean hill of delights. It is an indulgence and why not? It may have a short cropping season and occupy a lot of space, but there is nothing like it.

growing asparagus

Asparagus plants have sexes. Although female plants often make the fattest spears, they are less productive so it pays to go for the man. It is reasonably easy to grow asparagus from seed, but results are unpredictable and you must allow them three years to build up some stamina and stature before cropping them. It is far better to buy it in as crowns from a specialist. They will offer one-, two- or three-year-old plants: go for the three-year-olds, which will be a bit more expensive, but you can start eating them sooner – and that is the point. Establish a mutually beneficial relationship with your plants by watering them well as their fronds develop, and by feeding them with rotted muck, good compost or seaweed.

storing asparagus

If you only have a few plants you may need to store harvested spears until there are enough to make a worthwhile serving. Wrap them in a tea-towel and store them in the cool-box compartment in the fridge.

steam-boiling asparagus

When you come to cook the spears, rinse quickly to remove any earth. Because the base of the stems are coarser than the shoots, it is always best to steam asparagus upright, tied in loose bundles with string or garden twine, rather than boil them lying down where each part of the shoot will cook for the same time. There are special pans for this but if you don't have one just use the deepest pan you have and let your bundle lean against the side of the pan. Cook rapidly in a couple of inches of boiling slightly salted water and test for tenderness by sticking a sharp knife or skewer into the flesh of the base.

other cooking uses and methods

The slender spears of 'Verde', are an ideal addition to quiches, omelettes or soufflés and, if they are tender enough, can just be brushed sparingly with olive oil and grilled or barbecued. They need no pre-cooking if they have come straight from the garden.

the right moment – though that may be across several weeks. If you have picked spears at the right moment, their consistency should be similar throughout the stem, and although the base of the stem will always be a touch less tender than the growing tip, this is not a problem, since asparagus simply steamed is best eaten with the fingers and the base of the stem makes a convenient handle when dipping asparagus in butter or fresh mayonnaise.

choosing the asparagus to harvest

It is imperative not to pick all your asparagus spears. Sever one or two from each crown as you need them, but spread the harvest out over a few weeks. The plant needs to retain a number of growing shoots to help it build up strength. Always take the tallest stems when

'It is said that asparagus should never be cut for longer than six weeks.'

cutting asparagus

Spears are the new shoots of the asparagus plant, *Asparagus officinalis*, related to the lily family. Essentially they are a seaside plant and love well-drained sandy soil. Once asparagus is planted it likes to stay put and can occupy the same space for up to 20 years without deteriorating. The crowns that are sent out in spring are essentially a fat resting bud with a bunch of sprawling spidery roots attached. They are planted on ridges with the roots spread out on either side and soil is returned to tuck them in.

when to harvest asparagus

Harvest time is during late April, through May and into early June, depending on where you garden. Do not cut asparagus in the first two to three years after planting. It is said that asparagus should never be cut for longer than six weeks, although this time can be lengthened by growing different varieties, although not by much.

There should be no need for using 'old' asparagus. Because the plant makes a succession of growing shoots, they can all be harvested at

Time the cutting of each asparagus spear to the size at which you want to eat it and according to the way you are going to cook it.

When cutting asparagus, remove some of the soil gently by hand so you have a clear view of the base of the stem.

Cut the asparagus as close to the crown of the plant as possible without damaging it. You can buy a specialist knife, but a sharp kitchen knife will do.

harvesting. There is an optimum time before the end of the shoot starts to broaden and expand but after the stem has pushed itself out of the ground to give you a long, clean shoot.

how to cut asparagus

When harvesting, the idea is to cut off the spears as close to the crown of the plant as possible without damaging it. To that end specialist knives have been developed with a sharp v-shaped blade to straddle the stem and sever the spear as cleanly as possible. Such a tool is probably an essential only in the asparagus fields of Evesham and similar venues. No need for this unless you are thinking of going in for asparagus in a big way. A sharp kitchen knife will do. Removing some of the soil gently by hand gives a better view of what is happening. Plunge the blade between the spear and the plant, grasping the top of the spear with your other hand and making sure you don't cut into the plant's roots or other newer shoots.

steam-boiled asparagus

Steam-boiling is the easiest way of cooking asparagus: the stalks boil while the tips steam. There are a number of dressings to choose from on page 220.

serves 4

**2 bunches asparagus spears,
of similar diameter
sea salt
dressing of choice (see page 220)**

Tie the spears together with cotton thread, non-toxic string or a rubber band (note that the rubber band will stretch with the heat and go a bit slack).

Bring several pints of salted water to the boil. Place the bundles of asparagus upright against the side of a deep narrow pan with a lid. Fill the pan up to a couple of inches down from the start of the heads or tips. Get on to a rolling boil and cover with the lid.

Check for tenderness after 2 minutes by inserting a sharp knife into the stalk a few inches down from the head. Keep checking until tender, then pull out the bundles and drain well. Cut the restraints.

Open the spears out on to the serving dish and smother indulgently or scantily with the dressing of choice.

barbecued asparagus

Your own fresh-picked asparagus will have crisp stalks and a fair bit of sugar in them. Barbecuing will mobilize the sweetness and tenderize the stalks.

serves 4

**2 bunches young asparagus spears,
of similar diameter**

Get a barbecue rack or ribbed griddle pan hot – there is no need to oil it – and lay on the asparagus spears one deep, so you can turn them quickly.

Let the spears char slightly before turning gently to prevent burning.

Try to do them all round. This should only take a minute or two.

If your spears are fat or woody, don't have the rack too hot and maybe cover the spears with foil or a lid to steam them at the same time.

barbecued asparagus

cabbage family

broccoli

Broccoli can be both a tender delicacy eaten as tight-packed flower buds or tender sprouted shoots, or a stalwart component of winter and early spring cuisine. Broccoli is rich in phyto-chemicals, folic acid, Vitamins A, B_2 and B_6, phosphorus, calcium and iron, and it is high in fibre. All-round good news, and it tastes good too.

growing sprouting broccoli

Whichever broccoli you grow, its flavour is improved by cold weather, though when hard frost is forecast, cover the tops of plants with newspaper or old net curtains.

preparing sprouting broccoli

Sprouting broccoli needs little preparation: it should be picked as tender young shoots and used immediately to maintain its crispness, which is its huge delight.

cooking sprouting broccoli

Rapid cooking is a must for most brassicas, but especially important when it comes to any of the family where it is the flower buds and stems that are eaten. The first new shoots can be steamed briefly and eaten simply with butter or a splash of olive oil. They are also a delicious constituent of a quick stir-fry, and accompanied by ginger, garlic and soy sauce make a straightforward but satisfying adjunct to noodles. Young shoots of broccoli can be eaten raw as crudités, but the best time to enjoy them in this way is when they are in their infancy. Or they can be blanched for a couple of seconds, then plunged into cold water, when they will be as crisp and crunchy as carrots.

cooking other varieties of broccoli

The largest apical head of sprouting, or ordinary calabrese and other varieties of broccoli, can be pulled apart, stem from stem, for rapid cooking (stir-frying or steaming, adding to pasta or eating just as it is). Alternatively you can treat it as a cauliflower, steaming it whole and submerging it in sauce, something cheesily traditional or a little more exciting with an orangey tang (the two flavours work remarkably well).

eating sprouting broccoli (and other) seeds

Seed sown on damp tissue or in old punnets or egg-boxes on to a thin layer of compost will germinate rapidly and can be grown and cut just like cress. Sprouted vegetables like this are packed full of nutrition: the minerals and vitamins are concentrated so even tiny amounts are beneficial, and sprouts have none of the sulphurous connotations of broccoli and cauliflower. A ready supply of all kinds of seeds throughout the year means they can be strewn on all sorts of food. Seed of F1 hybrid cultivars would be an expensive proposition, as there are very few seeds in a packet, so go for fat packets of cheaper seed.

'Stems can be cut from the top downwards in succession, as each reaches its prime.'

A sprouting broccoli plant can grow over 1m (3ft) tall.

cutting broccoli and cauliflower

One of the huge clan of edible cabbages, *Brassica oleracea*, broccoli is part of the branch of the family whose flower heads are eaten. Cousins include calabrese, romanesco (whose taste doesn't live up to its sacred geometry), and cauliflowers, of which there are purple and white varieties all producing dense curds. Most of the brassicas – among them cabbages, cauliflowers, calabrese, sprouts and kale – are descended from the wild cabbage found in abundance around our seashores, usually on limestone cliffs.

In the garden, sprouting broccoli occupies a large area, but its impressive yield justifies its big footprint. Like all brassicas it loves decent soil, preferably on the alkaline side.

There is seldom room for more than a few plants of purple sprouting broccoli in the vegetable garden, but five or six plants will produce a big yield. A well-grown plant can grow over 1m (3ft) tall and may need staking in a windy site. As with all brassicas, firm planting is essential. Don't be scared of putting the boot in.

when to cut sprouting broccoli
Separate stems can be harvested over a long period and though they need a bit of elbow-room, the yield from a well-grown plant of purple sprouting broccoli, sown in March, transplanted in June and cropped from November to April, is impressively bountiful.

when to cut a cauliflower
It is possible to crop different cauliflowers through every month depending on your plot and locality. February and March are often thin months for crops, and November and December can bring the shock-realization that the season is over. So you can decide when you would

Separate stems can be harvested over a long period of time.

Sever individual stems from the top downwards in succession, as each reaches its prime.

most like to have cauliflowers around and work backwards from that.

how to cut sprouting broccoli

With all the sprouting varieties ('broccoli' means 'little sprouts' in Italian), stems can be cut from the top downwards in succession as each reaches its prime, so if there are several plants, a good haul can be had at fairly frequent intervals, ensuring the whole bunch is as fresh as can be. Sever the individual stems, each with its own florets, from the main stem using a sharp knife or a pair of secateurs. The largest apical head (the one at the top) can be harvested first.

Cutting regularly stimulates the plant to make further shoots so even if you have missed the boat slightly as far as adolescent shoots are concerned, it is worth harvesting slightly older shoots to promote new growth. These are ideal ingredients in winter soup and great with cheeses, such as blue cheese or Stilton.

how to cut a cauliflower

With most of the other brassicas (cauliflower, calabrese etc), the whole head is sliced off at one fell swoop, using a sharp knife. Once an individual has been harvested, the decapitated plant can be pulled up and, if it is disease-free, it can be composted, bashing it up beforehand.

steamed broccoli

It is most potently healthy – and delicious – when eaten with the minimum amount of cooking to make it digestible. The home-grower has access to the most tender florets that don't require much cooking anyway. For some reason, steaming seems to cook vegetables much more quickly than boiling in water. They become tender more quickly but still retain an *al dente* bite, whereas boiled vegetables tend to go from tough to soggy without warning. Steamed vegetables keep a brighter colour – it even intensifies – and fewer of the vitamins and minerals are lost to the cooking water.

serves 2–3
450g (1lb) purple sprouting broccoli florets
1–2 garlic cloves, peeled and thinly sliced
sea salt and black pepper

Place the florets into a steamer or steaming colander with the garlic and some seasoning.

Suspend the steamer over a pan with an inch of fast-boiling water in, keeping a lid on top tightly closed. After 2 minutes stop the heat and let the steaming coast to a stop without heat underneath.

Check the stalks for tenderness with a sharp knife while letting the florets relax for a minute or two.

steamed broccoli with lemon sauce

Broccoli and, later on in the season, calabrese (the one that looks like a green cauliflower), go well with lemony flavours. The almonds add a touch of mild sweetness.

serves 2
1 medium garlic clove
1 small pinch sea salt
½ tablespoon olive oil
55g/2oz butter or another tablespoon olive oil
½ teaspoon minced chilli
zest and juice of 1 lemon
150ml (5fl oz) hot water
1 handful spring flowering broccoli (about 750g/1¾lb)
1 tablespoon flaked almonds

Peel and mash up the garlic with the salt in a mortar and pestle. Add the oil and stir into an emulsion. Tip it into a pan on a medium heat and add the butter or oil and the chilli. When it is bubbling hot but not frying, add the lemon juice and stir it into a syrupy sauce (about 3 minutes), adding enough of the water to stop it drying out or burning. Keep it warm.

Place the florets into a steamer or steaming colander. Suspend the steamer over a pan containing an inch of fast-boiling, salted water, and cover. After 3 minutes stop the heat and let the water coast to a stop.

Check the stalks for tenderness with a sharp knife while letting the florets relax for a minute or two. Meanwhile, dry-fry or oven-roast the almonds to crisp and lightly brown.

Fold the broccoli, sauce, almonds and lemon zest together immediately before serving.

steamed broccoli with lemon sauce

cauliflower

Cauliflowers are descendants of *Brassica oleracea* and share the family preference for being very firmly rooted into the soil. Don't be afraid to use your foot to press new plants in at planting. Cauliflowers can be quite demanding to grow and will expose any neglect they have suffered, so to avoid embarrassment, be prepared to commit yourself to them.

growing cauliflowers

Cauliflowers need a long growing season and should not suffer water-stress by being deprived of moisture as they grow. Varieties that over-winter will take up a large footprint without delivering any crop until spring. All cauliflowers should be protected from frost on the heads, perhaps by a fleece hat, and through the growing season try to maintain the leaves around the head to protect the curds.

crop rotation

Crop rotation probably benefits brassicas more than any other crop. If you can grow them where legumes, such as peas and beans, were growing last year, the brassicas will benefit considerably. The soil will hopefully have been fed or manured last year with nitrogen fixed in the soil by the legumes. Fresh manure, however, tends to inhibit the formation of curd-heads. Adding lime might be necessary to get the soil ph to 6.5–7.5.

storing cauliflowers

Cauliflowers should not be picked until you are ready to cook them, as you can never restore their crispness. If you have to store them, keep them covered in their own leaves to stop them drying out. Cauliflowers freeze well, but it works best to break large curds up into small florets first to speed freezing and thawing.

boiling and steaming cauliflowers

Whole curds can sit in a pan of boiling water up to the level of the bottom florets. A lid on the pan will speed up the cooking as the top florets will steam. Separate florets are better off being steamed than boiled (unless you are quickly blanching them) because they can disintegrate and go mushy. Try acidulating the water first by squeezing in the juice of a quarter lemon.

other cooking methods

A little raw cauliflower, say for a raw crudité for dipping, is fine in moderation, but improves by having the sulphurous after-taste removed by blanching or light steaming. However, overcooking to make it soft enough to purée or for cauliflower cheese renders it dead. For harvesting, see pages 30–31.

poached cauliflower à la grecque

Traditionally cauliflowers in Britain were presented to the cook as a big heavy ball. However, from your own garden you can pick cauliflowers as miniature delicacies and save yourself the stress of taking the curds all the way to unblemished white maturity.

serves 4

2 medium cauliflowers
10 garlic cloves
1 shallot or small onion
1 lemon
450ml (16fl oz) olive oil
300ml (10fl oz) white wine
225ml (8fl oz) white wine vinegar
15–20 green or black peppercorns
4 bay leaves, torn in half
2 tablespoons fennel seeds (optional)

Break the cauliflowers into mouth-sized florets. Peel and smash or finely slice the garlic. Peel and slice the onion and slice the lemon into 5mm (¼in) discs.

Meanwhile, simmer the oil, wine and vinegar together in a pan. Put all the ingredients – except for the cauliflower – into the pot, bring to a light boil and shut down the heat. Drop in the cauliflower now and leave to soak.

The residual heat is probably enough to cook or blanch the pieces. If not, let the simmering continue for a few minutes more.

Take out the vegetables to stop any more cooking, and leave the liquid to cool down. When cold, return the vegetables to the liquid and serve cold the next day.

cauliflower with garlic & orange sauce

This orange sauce, given extra body from the butter and the garlic, counteracts the brassica flavour of the cauliflower with a sweet fruitiness.

serves 2

3 small cauliflower heads, or 1 large head, broken into large florets
1 medium garlic clove
1 small pinch sea salt
1 tablespoon olive oil
55g (2oz) butter or another tablespoon oil
½ teaspoon minced or finely cut fresh red chilli
juice of 1 large orange or 2 medium oranges
½ teaspoon grated orange zest
150ml (5fl oz) hot water

Steam the cauliflower in a steamer, or blanch in boiling water for 3 minutes, and set aside. Peel and smash the garlic in a pestle, first with the salt and then the oil.

Melt the butter or oil in a small pan and add the garlic mixture and the chilli. Stir them around but don't let them fry. Add the orange juice and stir into a syrupy sauce (about 4 minutes).

Roll the cauliflower around in the sauce so that it is all covered, even turning it upside down and spooning the sauce into the branches of the florets. Strew the orange zest over the cauliflower. Put a lid on the pan and continue cooking until the cauliflower is *al dente*, adding the water as necessary to prevent the sauce from drying out or sticking and burning.

cauliflower with garlic & orange sauce

leaves & herbs
spring herbs

Spring is all about jubilant growth, and the tender new shoots of wild sorrel, dandelion and garlic embody the freshness of the season. In the garden too, spring's herbs are tender and 'soft', which is what differentiates them from the more mature leaves of autumn and winter. It is well worthwhile growing your own, however modestly, as most commercial herbs are pale and tasteless in comparison. Providing you cut, water and feed them regularly (a balanced liquid organic seaweed feed once a week is very beneficial), you should be able to harvest well into the summer.

parsley Parsley should be sown at intervals from February onwards, although early crops will germinate better under cover. From mid-March they can be sown direct into the ground in rows or patches where nothing else is growing. They say if parsley germinates for you, then you wear the trousers. Want to make sure? Water in your seed with a kettle just off the boil. Parsley, whether curly or flat-leafed, needs to be cropped regularly to encourage the formation of new fresh leaves from the centre of the plant. Harvest the mature outer leaves, tender but substantial, cutting them close to the base.

chervil Chervil has open ferny leaves and a distinctly aniseed, slightly anaesthetic, tang. Harvest a few leaves at a time from the outside of the plant.

chives As a milder alternative to garlic and onions, chives are an important ingredient in the spring kitchen. They are the slender, scrolled leaves of a member of the onion family, best when young, the secret of eternal youth being to cut them continuously. The pretty pink flowers are edible too.

mint Mint is a perennial plant with running roots, giving a plentiful supply of young leaves. Plant in a pot and submerge this just below the level of the soil into a border or veg plot. There are multifarious varieties of mint, with perceptibly different flavours.

sorrel Sorrel has large leaves and is closely related to spinach. I love sharp acid tastes that stimulate your palate. Such is sorrel, so much so that it nearly makes your eyes water!

herb salad

Many salad crops are quite happy over-wintering and are ready to eat in early spring or have just started new growth. New spring herbs can re-energize these salads and lend refinement and interest.

serves as many as you can
mâche (lamb's lettuce)
chervil
oakleaf or cut-and-come-again lettuce
rocket (in moderation)
mizuna
chives (in moderation, and optional)
sorrel
garlic mustard or mustard leaves
  (in moderation)
dressing of choice (see page 220)

The mâche should be collected separately from the others because, if they do not need washing, the mâche certainly will. Swilling the leaves in clean, cold water will reveal a surprising diversity of wildlife that can go back on the garden. Mâche grows as a tight rosette that has soil trapped deep in its stalks. The leaves are a bit small to harvest individually so it is easier to handle the rosettes. These should be shaken under water, maybe even in a couple of changes of water. Wrapping all the leaves in a clean tea-towel and windmilling it over your head a few times dries them as well as anything.

Mix, dress sparingly and serve.

chervil butter

Chervil butter is a fresh and charming accompaniment to potatoes, carrots and legumes. On serving it looks very pretty and as it melts it maroons little flecks of chervil on the shiny vegetables.

makes 55g (2oz)
1 good handful chervil leaves
55g (2oz) pale unsalted butter, at room
  temperature

If necessary wash the chervil and shake off the water to leave it as dry as possible. Strip the leaves off the stems and chop finely, perhaps with a rocking hachoir.

Fold the leaves into the butter and pat into a serving dish. Refrigerate the dish to let the butter firm up before using.

herb salad

summer

peas, beans & sweetcorn

peas

We think of fresh peas as the epitome of summer eating: brief visitors to the table. Even in supermarkets, they are still fleetingly seasonal. (People point out that frozen peas, available all year long like tasteless strawberries, are a success story for industrial agriculture, but they only one variety is available.)

There are two kinds of peas in the kitchen: the young crisp sweet ones and the old floury cannonballs. It depends on the variety, but a spell of hot, dry weather can very quickly turn the first type into the second.

growing peas

Heritage varieties are worth experimenting with, as the cropping period for many peas is condensed into a few weeks in early summer. Not only are varieties markedly different, but their maturity at picking can be important. See Varieties, above.

cooking peas (and pea pods)

The impact of refined French petits pois on a Britain accustomed to mushy peas and hard-boiled cannonballs in the 1960s is still reverberating. Boil them briefly, then serve them with a little butter, or incorporate them into another dish, such as a risotto, omelette or frittata. You can purée them or serve them with herbs (particularly mint). You can make your own very classy mushy peas by puréeing older peas after boiling them soft, or go on to make a wonderful velvety soup.

eating pea pods

When you've shelled your youngest peas, you are left with a mountain of bright green pods. If you think they look good enough to eat, well they are. In fact, eating mangetout (juvenile peas in a pod) and the fatter sugar-snap version have led the way to eyeing up the whole plant as an edible opportunity.

cooking pea tips and shoots

Pea tips (the growing point or the unopened baby leaves) and the tendrils can be eaten as a garnish or in a stir-fry for an extra pea-tasting detail. They can be washed and quickly sautéed; the lingering droplets of water will keep them fresh and prevent frying.

Pea shoots are full of pea flavour, but are quite powerful. They are just sprouted peas started with no soil, only light, warmth and moisture, but they contain everything a pea plant will become. Assure yourself that the pea seeds are organic or at least not treated with some chemical preservative as you will be eating them directly from the plant.

'Because pods mature successively, it is important to harvest continuously.'

picking peas and beans

The wild predecessors of runner beans and climbing French beans are plants that need to clamber and climb, twisting and twining their way towards the light and wrapping themselves around any twig or branch to support themselves and pull themselves up. At the other end of the scale, dwarf French beans and broad or fava beans are bushy, freestanding plants that need no assistance. Somewhere in between, peas will scramble around, leaning on each other and helping themselves up with tendrils that gently, but opportunistically, attach themselves to wire, twigs or other peas.

The feature that all legumes share is the pod, within which their seeds are carried. Sometimes we eat the seeds, sometimes the pods, and occasionally both. Because the pods mature successively, it is important to harvest continuously to ensure a constant crop. In most cases this means picking pods when they are young enough to be tender but mature enough for their flavour to have fully developed.

When harvesting beans, support the fragile stem and pull the ripe pod firmly away from it.

how to pick peas and beans

Pods are securely attached to the plant and have to be detached by pulling them firmly away from the stems, but it is important when harvesting to ensure that the main stem is not damaged. If it is broken then the future of further flowers and pods will be in jeopardy. As you pull the pod from the plant, hold the stem firmly with your other hand to protect it.

how to pick french and runner beans

When harvesting runner beans and French beans it is sometimes easiest to nip them off beyond the pod with your thumbnail. Runner beans often have six or seven pods developing along one stem. Harvest them one or two at a time as they ripen. French beans should be harvested at the same stage.

Support the stem when removing the peas to avoid damaging the plant.

For haricot and other podded beans, allow them to dry on the stem a little before picking.

picking borlotti and haricot beans

If you are growing borlotti beans to dry and store for the winter, wait to harvest when the pods are dry and brown. Haricot beans can be dried too or eaten when they are ripe. Recipes abound for simple bean dishes and all these beans are rich in iron, potassium and vitamins.

picking peas

Peas are best picked as they just fill the pods when they are young and full of sugar. If you are picking for crispness, pick early and greedily. Polite caution is never rewarded by peas. The exception to this rule is if you are picking for storage, as our ancestors had to. Then you can let the peas fatten and dry in the pod.

To collect seeds for next year, leave the pods to dry fully on the stem.

riso con piselli

The rice and the peas are each cooked separately, then combined for serving. The rice cooks much more slowly and shouldn't be rushed or over-stirred because too much starch would be bullied out of the grains and the texture disappointing. The fresh peas cook in a trice and this helps keep their lovely colour bright.

serves 4

115g (4oz) unsalted butter
250g (9oz) Italian risotto rice,
    preferably carnaroli
sea salt and black pepper
700 mililitres (1¼ pints) water
225g (8oz) fresh shelled peas

In a pan with a lid, melt half of the butter and while it is still foaming, add the rice. Stir the rice with a mean pinch of salt until it goes translucent. Don't let the rice or the butter burn.

Stir in 700ml (1¼ pints) hot water and make sure all the rice grains are separate. Reduce the heat to next to nothing and put the lid on. About 8 minutes later, fork through the rice gently to check on cooking. Cook on slowly for another 10 minutes until *al dente*.

When it is 2 minutes away from being ready, put the peas in a new pan, cover with boiling water and bring to a fast boil for 2 minutes. The peas should be done, so drain them and fold them into the rice.

Serve with the rest of the butter and a generous grinding of black pepper.

mushy pea soup

There are always pea pods that escape picking and by the time you find them, the peas inside are pale, fat and squashed together. If your variety of pea has a fresh, full subtle flavour, keep the recipe purely peas. If they are a bit bland, soften a shallot in a little butter or oil in the pan first and add a few fresh mint leaves to the boiling peas.

serves 4

350g (12oz) floury, even mealy, peas
1.2 litres (2 pints) water
sea salt and black pepper
2 large handfuls pea shoots (optional)
115g (4oz) butter (optional)

Place the peas in a pan with the water and gently boil until soft, about 15 minutes. Liquidize the peas, adding enough hot water to get the thickness of soup you like (I like mine thick). Keep the soup hot and season lightly, as even old home-grown peas have a delicate flavour.

Shred the pea shoots and sauté them in the butter, adding a drop of water to stop them burning. Dish up the soup with the shoots as a garnish, if using.

mushy pea soup

VARIETIES

Some good broad beans are 'SUPER AGUADULCE' and 'AQUADULCE SUPERSIMONIA'.

broad beans

Broad beans are *Vicia faba*, or fava beans. Grown all over the world due to their reliable vigour, they are ideal for novice growers. They supply dramatic looks, a sweet scent and a meal for every stage of growth.

cooking and eating broad bean tips and pods

When the plants are well established and showing enough flower buds, it is good practice to nip out the upwards-facing cluster of baby leaves. (This denies blackfly, or black bean aphids, their favourite congregation place and helps prevent an infestation.) These broad-bean tips are a delicacy, either raw in salads, stir-fried or sautéed in a flash for a garnish. After the first flowers have set into little beans, the whole pod, until it is the size of a little finger, can be steamed or boiled. The pod can also be steamed if it is sliced through, diagonally for preference.

cooking (and freezing) young broad beans

Quickly the pod size grows away and becomes inedible. When you can just feel the beans inside the pod, you can harvest a few to eat the bright green juvenile beans as raw crudités or as an Italian-style appetizer with salt and olive oil. For a few days, you can cook them steamed or poached still in their skins in any recipe as you might use peas, they are so bright and tender.

When they are at this first cooking stage, consider freezing them. Ideally, lay them in a single layer and freeze as quickly as possible, after a minute's blanching in boiling water and an ice-bath to help with getting the skins off if you can be bothered.

cooking more mature broad beans

As maturity accelerates, the beans grow bigger and their skins get paler, thicker and a bit acrid if chewed. However, if you steam or boil them briefly, you can nick an opening in the skin and gentle squeezing will pop the bright green bean out nicely. For cold salads, a minute's blanching followed by an ice-cold plunging for another minute will arrest further cooking and safeguard the tender crispness.

The bean pods will start to get very fat. The lining of the pod is very thick, almost like a fleece-lined cocoon for the smooth shiny beans. The beans still look disconcertingly small considering the size of the pods, but that is no bad thing.

cooking mature and old broad beans

Within weeks the pods acquire a heavy coarseness, bulging with big beans inside. These beans will definitely need their skins peeled and the bright green translucent crispness will have given way to a more opaque pale green luminescence. This is a substantial bean ready for more robust cooking. It is slightly floury and very mild in flavour.

Pods left dangling through summer will start to look very blemished and the puffiness inside will have started to shrink. The beans inside will be harder and more solid and less attractive to cook with – a bean for soups, stews and ragoûts. You'll wish you had eaten them all when they were immature.

broad bean risotto

Young broad beans can go in the rice and pea recipe (see page 50), and peas can go in this more robust bean recipe.

serves 4

5 spring onions or 1 baby leek, chopped
100g (3½oz) butter
250g (9oz) basmati or long-grain rice
sea salt and black pepper
700ml (1¼ pints) water, boiling
1 bunch fresh parsley, chopped
1 pinch saffron strands (optional)
175g (6oz) young podded broad beans
1 bunch fresh dill, chopped

In a pan, stew the onions or leek in the butter until soft, about 5 minutes, then stir in the rice with a pinch of salt. Add most of the boiling water when all the grains are coated with butter and stir to separate them. Add the parsley and a teacup of water containing the saffron, if using, put on a lid and remove from the heat. Leave to sit for 10 minutes, by which time the rice should have cooked by itself.

Steam the beans in a steamer, or cover with boiling water for 4 minutes, and test them for tenderness. Check to see if the rice is done, starting up the heat again and adding more water if necessary.

Drain the beans and add to the rice with the dill and some more salt and pepper to taste.

broad bean salad

Young broad beans are best for a salad, but older ones can be very nearly as good, as long as you don't mind peeling off the bitter skins. You can take the skin off before or after boiling for about 4 minutes. Make a nick in the side of the pod with a sharp knife and squeeze the beans out. Cold beans could be served on a bed of raw pak-choi leaves and older beans mixed with baby beetroots (see variation below).

Serves 2

2 handfuls pak choi leaves
85g (3oz) young podded broad beans
pak choi flowers, to garnish

Arrange the pak choi leaves on 2 plates, divide the broad beans between them and garnish with the pak choi flowers.

Variation

Serves 2

6 baby beetroots
85g (3oz) young podded broad beans
balsamic vinaigrette made with 3 tablespoons olive oil and 1 tablespoon balsamic vinegar
sea salt and black pepper

Boil the beetroots for about 10 minutes, and test for tenderness with a sharp knife. Cool them under cold water, then top, tail and peel them.

Boil or steam the beans for about 4 minutes.

Chop the cool beetroot into 2.5cm (1in) chunks and mix in with the beans. Dress with the balsamic vinaigrette and season to taste.

broad bean salad

french beans

French beans are tender, but when they get going they are strong and vigorous. The plants are not as rampant as runner beans, but the beans are much more refined and versatile. Although there are perfectly good dwarf bush varieties, the climbing varieties look very attractive laden with hanging pods. There are green, yellow, purple and freckled varieties ('Rampicante Supermarconi' is shown opposite).

cooking young french beans

French beans can be collected while they are still very small, as short as your little finger and as thick as a fat matchstick. Freshly picked, these *haricots vert* only need blanching for 20 seconds to get them thoroughly hot. If this smacks of infanticide, let them grow on to the size of a short skinny pencil. One or two minutes' steaming is sufficient for *al dente*, then leave them in the steamer without heat for another minute for tender but not soft.

cooking more mature french beans

When the pods lose their crispness and become knobbly, it is better to leave them growing for a while as their suddenly coarse texture is a disappointment. Firm, hard lumps inside the pod tell you it's viable to shell (or shuck) them to get the bright little beans out. These can be treated like fresh peas: they don't have the puckered skin like broad beans do after cooking.

Later the pods will become leathery and fibrous, the beans inside bulging and dense. This is the time of the perfect flageolet: mature and flavoursome, but not yet hard and dry. These flageolets can be cooked separately by boiling briefly in salted water, then added to recipes. (Confusingly, these green flageolets can be dried in this green state. Once dried, they will need pre-cooking by simmering in salted water for anything between 3 and 30 minutes, depending on variety and maturity.)

storing and cooking dried french beans

By the end of summer, the pods will be brown and withered, the beans inside as hard as pebbles. They will have dried out naturally and protected themselves in a smooth shiny skin, pale-cream-coloured as haricots, or splashed with crimson as borlotti. Pick them on a warm, dry day and lay them out for an hour, then you can store them for the winter in glass jars if your kitchen isn't steamy – or better still, freeze them.

Haricots and borlotti, like the similar cannellini and lima beans need soaking for several hours (or overnight) and cooking in their own water before being added to recipes.

french beans in yoghurt & walnut sauce

When they are ready, French beans quickly become the first choice vegetable for all sorts of meals, hot or cold.

serves 4
1 garlic clove, peeled
sea salt
40g (1½oz) shelled walnuts
400g (14oz) Greek-style yoghurt
1kg (2¼lb) French beans, topped

In a pestle if available, grind the peeled garlic into a paste with a little salt.

If the walnuts taste stale or bitter, soak them in boiling water for 10 minutes, discarding any loose skin. Break up the drained walnuts and grind into the garlic paste. Scrape the mixture out of the pestle and fold into the yoghurt.

Steam the topped beans for 5 minutes (you don't need to tail home-grown beans) in a steamer.

Fold the beans into the yoghurt and serve.

french bean salad

New French beans have a delicate flavour that can be swamped by big recipes. Like fresh peas, they deserve to be eaten very simply without too many distractions.

serves 2–4
450g (1lb) French beans (different varieties, if available)
sea salt and black pepper
1 tablespoon extra virgin olive oil
juice and zest of ½ lemon

Nip off the top stalks of the beans and steam over a rolling boil for 3 or 4 minutes, or boil in deep, lightly salted water for 4 or 5 minutes, until *al dente*.

Drain, run under cold water and drain again.

Drizzle on the oil and squeeze the lemon over them all, season with salt and pepper, and lightly toss with the lemon zest.

french bean salad

runner beans

Runner beans are no slouchers: when they get going after the last frosts there is no stopping them. Growing as climbers, they are soon covered in a relentless succession of beautiful red, pink or white flowers, even late into the season. Nearly every flower will become a bean. Picking regularly, and this means every day, can ensure fresh young beans from midsummer to mid-autumn.

THE FIVE STAGES OF GROWING AND COOKING RUNNER BEANS

Runner beans should get plenty of water at their roots especially as they must support easily 1kg (2¼lb) of succulent pods per plant.

Provided there have been enough insects to pollinate the flowers, and pods have set, you can expect your runner beans to go through five main stages of development:

stage 1 There is a flat skinny pod about 7.5cm (3in) long. That's not worth picking if you also have French beans on the go.

stage 2 The pod is now about 18cm (7in) long and decidedly flat, about a finger's width wide. Check for side strings. These pods can be cooked whole or snapped in half with a satisfying crack into boiling salted water. They will probably take about 3 minutes to get just to the other side of *al dente*. These are a delight with a yielding texture and a disarmingly fresh but full flavour.

stage 3 It's now or never, the pod is about 23cm (9in) long and about as wide as your thumb, still mainly flat, but with a few low bumps just discernible. You will have to try pulling any strings off both sides, resorting to a blade if necessary. These pods can be snapped in three or cut diagonally on the bias and steamed for maybe 4 minutes.

stage 4 At this stage, you've almost lost it. The pods are an inch or two longer but you can see the beans inside bulging. The skin has a fibrous texture and the strings come off like skinny flat shoe-laces. At this point you can still eat them as sliced pods, cutting right through the beans too, but the danger is that by the time the rough outside of the pod is digestible, they will look khaki-coloured, not bright green.

stage 5 Now you have lost it. The pods are 30cm (12in) plus, coarse looking and bulging with beans inside. Either let them grow on to save and swap the seed, or cut your losses and pick them and compost them, which will encourage new bean formation.

how to pick and eat runner beans Your beans will not all mature together simultaneously, but there will always be enough of them to make a picking. The reality is that you will only discover the big beans when they are upon you. My advice is don't use up all the big ones first because by the time the next picking comes around, the little ones will now be giants as well. If you feel sorry for them, you will end up only ever eating coarse, hulking great runner beans.

runner bean frittata

Runner beans are a reliable and prolific crop, but the beans can easily overtake your consumption. Rather than try to catch up by going back to the biggest ones that got away, it's better to cut your losses and start again with nice-sized ones – flat and smooth, not bulging with mature beans inside. If you're having beans at every meal, this is a nice change.

serves 4–6

500g (18oz) runner beans, topped
4 large or 6 small eggs
1 bunch fresh parsley, leaves only, chopped
1 small bunch fresh chives, chopped
sea salt and black pepper
juice and zest of 1 lemon (optional)
55g (2oz) butter
1 tablespoon extra virgin olive oil

Preheat the oven to 200°C/400°F/Gas 6.

Steam the beans until tender, about 5 minutes, then drain and chop into 5cm (2in) lengths. Keep hot.

Whisk the eggs in a bowl and add the chopped parsley and chives with a pinch of salt. If using, add the lemon zest and as much lemon juice as you fancy.

In a frying pan melt the butter in the oil and when it is foaming add the egg mixture. Add the beans and cover them with the still runny egg mixture.

Cook until the underside is set and it seems to be cooking around the edges, then put it into the hot oven or under a moderate grill to cook the top, for about 4 or 5 minutes.

runner beans with harissa paste

If you have to take off tails and strings from the length of your beans you are growing a boring variety – try another next year. If your chillies are only selected for heat rather than piquancy you won't taste the beans.

serves 4–6

675g (1½lb) runner beans, too young to feel proper beans inside the pod
sea salt
2–3 tablespoons harissa paste (see page 146)
plain yoghurt (optional)

Nip off the top stalks of the beans. Snap the beans into manageable lengths, about 7.5cm (3in) long. Put in a steamer over a rolling boil for 3 or 4 minutes, or in deep boiling, salted water for 4 or 5 minutes until *al dente*.

Drain the beans and dress with the harissa in the pan or a serving bowl. (Plain yoghurt mixed into the harissa will calm it down a little.)

runner beans with harissa paste

VARIETIES

The only alternatives to **'SUGARY ENHANCED'** and **'SUPERSWEET'** F1 hybrids offered to the grow-your-own gardener are the less uniform, modestly yielding heritage varieties such as **'DOUBLE STANDARD'**, **'ASHWORTH'** or **'GOLDEN BANTAM'**.

Otherwise, if you can handle it, stick to **'NORMAL SUGARY'**, and don't let your seed-dealer push you on to sweeter and sweeter corn.

sweetcorn

The fresh sweetness of sweetcorn is fragile and very elusive, but this hasn't stopped man from seeking it. Flour ground from maize was the Aztecs' staple food. The kernels were as pretty as beads, a mad mix of white, yellow, beige, orange, red, brown, purple, blue and black. The Hopi and Seneca tribes revered their corn, and 'Seneca Red Stalker' (with purple-red husks) and 'Hopi Blue' sweetcorn (used to make blue tortillas) are still available as heirloom seeds in America.

cooking sweetcorn

Put your pan of water on to boil before you go out to the garden to collect your corn-on-the-cob. Every minute after you have picked them, their sugar starts turning into starch, so you must cook them quickly to keep them sweet. Quickly boiled in unsalted water for 5 or so minutes, checking for tenderness by taking off a kernel and biting it, sweetcorn only needs to be slathered in the best butter you can find.

big business and sweetcorn

Nathaniel Stowell of New Jersey bred 'Stowell's Evergreen Sweet Corn' in 1848, dying in poverty as others became rich from it. In 1900, Atlas Burpee bought a bucket of 'Golden Bantam' kernels – Burpee has since become a giant US horticultural corporation. Sweetcorn connoisseurs regard these two as still having the best flavour and balance between sugar, starch and the magic ingredient of flavour no one can capture.

Sweetcorn plant-breeding has been taken away from gardeners and taken over by big business. First there was 'Normal Sugary', then 'Sugary Enhanced' with increased sugar levels, then 'Supersweet' or technically 'Shrunken-2' – even sweeter but with a crispy rather than creamy texture and smaller, lighter, shrunken kernels that retain moisture and therefore shelf-life for longer. Saving seeds for home gardeners is not the breeders' priority; hybrids between undisclosed parents are sold annually, with no scope for the gardener to keep and re-sow their favourites or select their own. Corn-syrup production has overtaken both cane and beet sugar. Now, with genetic modification of corn in the heavily subsidized US market, production of ethanol for biofuel from the syrup has passed 40 per cent. GM corn is penetrating all global markets outside Europe.

'From the minute it is harvested, its sugar will turn to starch. So, take it at the last possible moment.'

An indication of when sweetcorn is ready to harvest is the tassels at the end of the cob turning dry and brown.

picking sweetcorn

Sweetcorn is a glorified grass, and the cobs that we value so highly are the seeds gathered together and clustered around a stem. All grasses are wind pollinated rather than their pollen being disseminated by insects, as is the case with the majority of our fruit- or seed-bearing vegetables.

growing sweetcorn

For the above reason, it is best to plant sweetcorn in a block rather than a line: the chances of the male pollen, which is borne at the top of each stem, hitting the female flowers (the tassels halfway down the stem) are greatly increased by the corn being planted in a matrix. Eventually, the seed from the female 'flower' will start to swell and form the cob surrounded by a paper covering.

Most plants produce at least two cobs, some as many as four. If you have grown an F1 hybrid variety, cobs will mature at the same time. It is difficult to avoid a glut.

With most crops, successional sowing would be the answer, but with sweetcorn that might defeat the object of the exercise, since you need them all to flower at the same time for effective pollination. Using an open-pollinated variety (seeds are always cheaper and there are lots more of them – you can even save your own) will give you more random results and therefore prolong cropping time. Or sow in two smaller blocks, starting a second lot of seed and planting out two weeks later.

when to harvest sweetcorn

One of the most asked questions in veg growing is 'How can I tell if my sweetcorn is ready to harvest?' The tassels at the end of each cob eventually turn dry and brown. Pull back the papery covering gently to expose the cob. If the seeds are a good yellow colour and look quite plump, plunge a thumbnail into one

Pull back the papery covering gently, to expose the cob. The colour of the kernels will tell you if the sweetcorn is ready to be harvested.

Ripe sweetcorn kernels should be bright yellow, firm and succulent.

of them close to the top. If a milky liquid comes out, then the sweetcorn is ready to be eaten. If the kernels are still dry, wait a few days.

From the moment it is harvested, its sugar will turn to starch. So, take it at the last possible moment.

how to harvest sweetcorn

The only implements you need when picking corn are your hands. Grasp the main stem firmly with one hand and the sweetcorn with the other, and pull the latter downwards, snapping the stalk that attaches it.

Push a thumbnail into a kernel – milky liquid should come out of it if it is ready to eat.

barbecued sweetcorn

Sweetcorn cannot be bettered simply boiled and served with fresh butter. If you want to vary it, sweetcorn can be barbecued very well. Don't strip the leaves from the cob but use them to protect the kernels from the fire and allow the barbecue flavour to get in.

per person
1 sweetcorn cob
**1–2 tablespoons melted butter or marinade
of choice**

You can go further than butter when barbecuing sweetcorn, of course. A contrast to the sweetness of the corn can be a sour or salty and savoury marinade, but it doesn't need to be overpoweringly strong. Harissa paste (see page 146) can be smeared on sparingly for a hot, chilli contrast. A dressing of an emulsion of garlic crushed into olive oil with sea salt can be worked into the gaps. This dressing can be given a light sour note by adding the juice of a lime or even a sharper kick with lemon juice. A stickier dressing can be created by working a tablespoon of tamarind paste into the garlic emulsion. An Italian flavour can be given by brushing the corn with basil pesto or a concentrated tomato sauce (see pages 132 and 128).

In most versions, the cob should be snapped off the plant. Then, more carefully than usual, the papery leaves should be peeled back one at a time and lightly folded down to expose the kernels. Remove the silky strings and coat the kernels all the way round with the marinade. Return the leaves in the same order you unpeeled them. Twist them to tighten them around the cob. You can now barbecue the cobs for 5–10 minutes, turning as necessary. If the leaves are thin or in short supply, wrap the cobs in foil first.

sweet & sour sweetcorn salsa

This is a sweet and sour salsa, where you balance the sweetness of the sweetcorn with the sourness of the tomato. This can be reinforced by pomegranate seeds and balsamic vinegar with nasturtium seeds or even shredded chilli giving some heat.

serves 4
handful baby tomatoes
1 large sweetcorn cob
5–10 nasturtium seeds, to taste
seeds of ½ pomegranate (optional)
sea salt
balsamic vinegar, to taste (optional)

Cut the tomatoes in half in the serving dish to save the juice.

Boil the cob in a pan of fast-boiling deep water for 3 or 4 minutes. Drain and scrape the kernels off the cob with a sharp knife.

Drain off the excess water and stir the sweetcorn into the tomatoes, adding the nasturtium seeds and the pomegranate seeds, if using. Season with salt and balsamic vinegar, if using.

sweet & sour sweetcorn salsa

VARIETIES

There are numerous varieties of artichokes and, although most can be used for all recipes, each has its own special characteristics. If you have room you can grow more than one variety and, since they mature at different times, they can be harvested over a longer period.

'ROMANESCO', tinged with purple, and **'GREEN GLOBE'** mature later here than they would in warmer climes, but are just as tender when harvested promptly.

'VERT DE LYONS' is a famous French artichoke with good, fleshy calyces and a delicious flavour.

perennials

globe artichokes

Artichokes are perennial plants and although they take up a lot of space they are dramatically decorative in any part of the garden, paying a double dividend. Globe artichokes are flower buds that would eventually open out as large mauve thistles. Full-blown artichokes equals tough artichokes though, and you should always cut them when they are young and tender. Often the flower head will produce several flowers on each stem, but cut the apical flower first. This is the main one in the centre, which is always the first and the biggest.

steaming/boiling artichokes

Globe artichokes can be eaten as hearts (the insides of the immense flower heads with all the coarse outside leaves of the calyx pared away) or cooked whole in their youth, steamed/boiled until the base of the calyx petals is tender. Pull off a petal to try, holding it by its tip and pulling off the juicy flesh between your teeth. When you have finished eating, everybody's plate will be piled high with the debris of the feast but, before this, the ritual of pulling off each petal and dipping it into butter or dressing needs to be savoured.

stewing/deep-frying artichoke hearts

The babiest of baby hearts can be stewed whole or deep-fried. Older artichokes too can be stewed whole in oil (having trimmed back the petals), though they will take hours rather than minutes to cook. They can also be stewed whole in white wine and oil.

other cooking methods

Although in England and France artichokes are usually eaten steamed or boiled, in Italy and California there are a plethora of techniques for cooking them, and if you grow your own, they will be fresh enough to give you the option of experimenting. Stew them in oil, slice them and bake them in cream and Parmesan with a sprinkling of thyme, or slice them raw into salads. In my youth I lived in the Jewish quarter in Rome for a year and the most memorable pizzas were the ones smothered in slices of artichokes, potatoes and chunks of hard-boiled eggs that were handed out to pavement level from a basement pizzeria.

'Every cut surface of the artichoke will oxidize quickly and turn grey. Submerging it swiftly in acidulated water – in other words, water with lemon juice or vinegar added – or wiping it with a lemon is necessary.'

preparing globe artichokes

very young globes

When the artichoke bud is very young it is a tight ball about the size of a large hen's egg. A few leaves around the bottom can be peeled off if they seem tough, and the stem can be cut off to leave a flat base, or left on with the skin pared off. The globe can be cut into flat discs about 5mm (¼in) across and used raw or blanched in a salad. It can also be cooked whole.

more mature globes

Young artichokes then grow into the size of a tennis ball, with the bottom leaves opening out and beginning to toughen up. The top leaves are beginning to fold their tips into sharp points. By hand, the stem can be snapped off and the bottom ring or two of leaves ripped off firmly. The pointy tips have to go, so there are two routes to take.

for quarters and hearts

For an Italian dish of cooked artichoke hearts, slice through the tough part of the leaves at the top of the globe. You can now cut the globe into quarters. You may see some hairy fibres called the choke in the middle and these can be pulled out with your fingers or scraped out

A young artichoke can be cooked whole with a few leaves peeled off. More mature ones, where the bottom leaves have opened out, need their outer leaves peeling off.

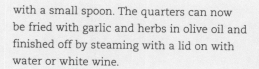

For a dish of artichoke hearts, cut through the tough part of the leaves from the outer to the inner ones, then cut the globe into quarters.

Pull the choke out from the heart with your fingers or scrape away with a spoon.

with a small spoon. The quarters can now be fried with garlic and herbs in olive oil and finished off by steaming with a lid on with water or white wine.

for globes to stuff and strip

For an Anglo-French dish of plucked and sucked leaves, dipped in lemon butter or dressing, the top of the globe is cut right across, flat. The soft but papery centre is opened in the middle and pulled back. A dessert or large teaspoon is inserted into the centre and worked around in a circle to sever the hairy choke, which is chucked. You can return the disc of little leaves to the globe; if you turn it upside down first, it can hold the dressing like a cup.

The cut artichokes will quickly turn grey when they are exposed to oxygen. To avoid this, submerge them in water with lemon juice squeezed in.

globe artichoke buds with garlic & lemon

Growing your own globe artichokes gives you a chance to eat them at a tender age that is not available commercially, and in a quantity that would be prohibitively expensive. This recipe takes advantage of the immature buds.

serves 2

1 panful small artichoke buds, maybe a dozen
juice of 1 lemon
3 garlic cloves, peeled and crushed
2 glugs olive oil, about 75ml (2½fl oz)
1 tablespoon chopped fresh thyme or parsley
225ml (8fl oz) water
1 pinch each of sea salt and black pepper

Trim the artichokes and store in a bowl of water with a small squeeze of lemon juice. When ready to use, drain.

Put all the ingredients except the remaining lemon juice into a wide pan with a lid. Put on a medium heat and simmer with the lid on for 5–10 minutes. Gently agitate the buds to even out the heat during this cooking.

When the buds are almost tender, turn up the heat to reduce the liquor, lid off. (Take the buds out during this operation if they are in danger of overcooking and disintegrating.)

Adjust the seasoning and add lemon juice to taste. Return the buds to their liquor.

stuffed niçoise globe artichokes

This is a recipe for the more mature artichoke. Follow the preparation guide on pages 72–3 to cut the artichoke straight across.

serves 4

1 onion or 2 shallots, peeled and sliced
4 garlic cloves, peeled and crushed
2 tablespoons fresh thyme leaves
2 tablespoons olive oil
85g (3oz) pitted black olives (Niçoise type)
100ml (3½fl oz) white wine
1 pinch each of sea salt and black pepper
4 large artichokes
2 large ripe tomatoes, finely diced
115g (4oz) dry breadcrumbs
finely grated zest of 1 lemon
1 teaspoon balsamic vinegar
2 tablespoons chopped fresh parsley

Preheat the oven to 180°C/350°F/Gas 4.

Gently stew the onion, garlic and thyme in the oil until the onions are soft and translucent, about 5 minutes, taking care not to let the garlic brown. Add the olives to heat through along with the wine, and test the seasoning.

Spoon ½ tablespoon of this mixture into each artichoke and spread the rest in an ovenproof dish. Stand the artichokes on this bed and fill them with a mixture of the tomato, breadcrumbs and zest. Turn them over so the bases are uppermost, and splash with the balsamic vinegar and some more olive oil.

Cover the dish with a lid or foil and bake in the preheated oven for an hour. Check to see if the artichokes are tender with a sharp knife, otherwise carry on baking. Turn them over on to their bases and scatter with the parsley.

stuffed niçoise globe artichokes

VARIETIES

COURGETTES 'VERDE DI MILANO' or the 'NANO' version both have good flowers. The light and dark striped 'STRIATO DI NAPOLI' and especially the dark-green types such as 'VERDE DI MILANO' need just a little bit more growth, to about 7.5cm (3in) and over, to find their sweetness. There are completely round courgettes that, once their flower-ends have been cut flat, are ideal for stuffing, such as 'TONDO DI TOSCANO', 'TONDO DI PIACENZA' and 'ROND DE NICE'. Yellow-skinned courgettes like 'PARADOR' and 'TAXI' can be used as green ones, but the immature flesh is denser and they slice brilliantly.

SUMMER SQUASHES Good ones include 'SUMMER CROOKNECK', which has a bright yellow, knobbly, almost warty skin, dense flesh and a nutty flavour, and 'EARLY PROLIFIC STRAIGHTNECK', which is even more bountiful.

summer squash

courgettes & other summer squashes

'Courgette' is the French name and 'zucchini' the Italian name for the baby fruits of *Cucurbita pepo*, which, in English, mature into marrows. Summer squashes are also in this family and are eaten as babies, either raw or cooked, like courgettes, otherwise they grow huge and ultimately inedible. Courgettes are generally bred to have thin skins when young, and marrows are bred not to go too woolly when mature.

growing courgettes Courgettes are very vigorous plants and, if conditions are right, will yield plentiful crops over several months. The plants can exhaust themselves, but a continuous supply is possible by staggering seed-sowing every month from early spring to midsummer. Young plants cannot stand any frost, but may be started off under cover. Although there are trailing and bush types, expect a courgette plant to occupy about a square yard.

cooking courgettes The mild flavour and easy-going texture of courgettes make them easy to use, but these can be carelessly abused by fast-boiling in water or burning in oil that is too hot. Gently does it. Very often older, overgrown courgettes, gathered together later in the summer, are chopped up with reject tomatoes, aubergines and peppers, and turned into self-confessed ratatouille. (How much nicer to use small young fruits with the first of the tomatoes.) It freezes well when cooked, cooled and quickly frozen. When this is resurrected in midwinter with a crumbling of frozen marjoram or basil, memories of summer days come flooding back.

cooking summer squash Summer squashes used very young can be treated and cooked just like courgettes. Their juvenile skin is nearly as tender but, as they grow away, it toughens, and they become more awkward to cook with.

'A courgette left too long will rapidly change into a prize marrow and, since we are growing to eat and not for the village show, cutting should be a daily event.'

It is advisable to harvest courgettes daily – they are at their peak for a short time and quickly mature into marrows.

cutting courgettes and summer squash

The courgette is one of the easiest and most satisfying crops to harvest. It must be done assiduously: a courgette left too long will rapidly change into a prize marrow.

harvesting courgette flowers

Plants bear both male and female flowers. The female is easy to identify as it always has an embryonic fruit to which the flower is joined. Once this flower has done its job and has been pollinated by a passing bee, it will collapse and fall, and the fruit will begin to swell. Male flowers hang around longer and it is these we snap off to stuff with rice, vegetables and pine nuts, or cheese and herbs, or to deep-fry.

when to harvest courgettes and summer squash

When courgettes are really tiny, barely a day old, they still have a stickiness about them; at this stage their taste has not developed fully. A day later the fruit has quadrupled in size, pumped full of water from the earth; it has lost its stickiness, though the skin is still meltingly soft. From this stage on and for the next two days, both courgettes and summer squash are at their best. Harvesting should be a daily event. Even if you do not need all the fruit that are ready at a particular time, it is still best practice to pick them all at the right stage.

how to cut courgettes

Harvesting young courgettes could not be easier. The fruit is attached to the plant with a short, ribbed stem; simply sever this with a small, sharp knife, taking care not to wrench it from the plant.

storing courgettes

Gather young fruits together in a basket or box, lining it with leaves (or even weeds), so that the slightly tacky, thin-skinned fruit is protected.

When harvesting, use a sharp knife to sever the courgette at its short ribbed stem, taking care not to wrench it from the plant.

Older fruits can be stored in the crisper compartment of the fridge for several days or left in a cool place, preferably wrapped in a damp tea-towel.

cutting and storing mature summer squash and marrows

If fruit has been allowed to ripen further, the procedure for cutting is identical. Marrows and ripened squash can be stored in a cool larder for months. When they have been severed from the plant, leave them on the ground in an open position, inverting them so that the underside gets a chance to ripen. Bring them in if rain threatens and store when thoroughly dry, allowing air to circulate around each of them.

Marrows are cut in exactly the same way as courgettes, and are bred not to go too woolly when mature.

foamed & grated courgettes

Courgettes crop and cook brilliantly, but their very reliability leads some people to get bored with them. But every day brings a new courgette to the kitchen, as innocent and fresh as the first one. Celebrate the bounty but don't forget to marvel at the beneficence with this simple recipe.

serves 2

2 fresh courgettes, ideally the dark-green-skinned ones
55g (2oz) best pale unsalted butter

Using the coarse side of a cheese grater, grate the courgettes.

Gently melt the butter in a pan with a lid. Add the grated courgettes and close the lid. Agitate the pan to turn the courgettes. After about 2½ minutes, you should have a mound of steaming courgette and a pool of perfect green foamy liquor.

You can now serve the two separately as a vegetable and a broth with a little extra hot water or together as a moist dish on its own. The foam could be used in a gargouillou (see page 92), because it is the very essence of courgette.

courgettes with pine nuts, onions & raisins

Pine nuts and raisins are a classic combination that goes well with many vegetables, but perhaps best with courgettes.

serves 4

1 large onion, peeled
50ml (2fl oz) olive oil
sea salt
6 medium or 8 small courgettes
½ fennel bulb (optional)
115g (4oz) raisins
2½ tablespoons light sherry
55g (2oz) pine nuts, toasted

Put the raisins in the sherry to soak before you do anything else.

Chop the onion finely and stew gently in the oil with a pinch of salt for about 10–12 minutes.

Top and tail the courgettes and wipe the tiny bristles off. Slice them lengthways in thin slices. Slice the fennel into thin slices, if using.

When the onions are all soft and half in this world and half in the next one, take out of the pan and set aside. Add the fennel, if using, to the pan on a medium-high heat and after 3 minutes add the courgettes. Toss them regularly to separate the slices.

When the sugar in the courgettes starts turning them brown, add the onions, pine nuts, raisins and sherry. When the courgettes have all gone a bit translucent and medium-soft and the liquor has reduced, let the pan rest for a few minutes with a lid on.

courgettes with pine nuts, onions & raisins

VARIETIES

Early croppers are **'EARLY WONDER'** and **'BIKORES'** or the cylindrical **'FORANO'** and **'CARILLON'**.

Yellow-fleshed **'BURPEE'S GOLDEN'** and white **'BLANKOMA'** avoid the staining that occurs with red beetroot.

Another good one is **'BOLTARDY'**, and the striking red-leaved **'BULL'S BLOOD'**.

roots

beetroot

Beetroot is an all-round super-veg. It grows quickly in all soils, with decorative but delicious leaves, from a root that is very nutritious to eat young and is reliable to keep into winter when mature. Its image has enjoyed something of a makeover in recent years – going from an earthy soup and pickling ingredient to a modern salad ingredient.

growing beetroot

It takes less than two months to produce cute little roots and a pinch of baby leaves. You can sow a little cluster of seeds every couple of weeks and gamble on the weather. Beetroot is quick to bolt, and conventional gardeners would wait until midsummer to sow the seed. This is fine if you only want mature main-crop beetroot for winter storage, but you will deny yourself the pleasure of young salad beetroot.

harvesting beetroot

Baby beetroot usually need thinning and this is a harvesting opportunity. Micro-leaves are worth eating as a salad garnish in their own right or they can be left to grow on into tiny plants. All parts are edible after washing and a little judicious cleaning up.

Immature roots are worth taking out for eating at any stage. However, if you don't like raw or unpeeled beetroot, you will have to cook them, so it is better to wait until they are a manageable size. By the time they are bigger you have a proper crop anyway.

preparing beetroot

Beetroot bleed their purple-red stain easily, but by the same token it is water-soluble. (Try varieties that are not red, see above.) Avoid piercing or bruising the skin prior to cooking. Before cooking, the taproot can be shortened by cutting using the nail of the thumb and your forefinger and the leaves can be twisted off as a bunch, decisively, an inch or two above the root. Once cooked, the skin slips off very easily and the bottom taproot and the stalk top end slice off without resistance.

eating and cooking beetroot leaves

Young leaves are tender enough to be eaten raw in salads, where the red veins and stalks add interest and colour. Salads that would have too much beetroot sweetness can be adjusted by adding sorrel leaves for sourness or spinach leaves for balance; these three combined are a classic French leaf salad, or they can be steamed for a minute.

eating and cooking beetroot

Beetroot themselves can be eaten raw too. They are best peeled, though. Grating or shredding makes them more digestible. Beetroot can be steamed or boiled in a pan when tiny, or baked slowly in a roasting tin (some people wrap them in foil) with hot water added to the bottom to prevent burning.

beetroot & potato soup

Beetroot can take robust cooking: roasted with garlic and herbs or smokily barbecued in foil are good methods. Boiled or, better still, baked in the oven, your own home-grown beetroots take surprisingly little cooking to reach tenderness.

serves 4
1kg (2¼lb) beetroots
1 large floury potato
1 large onion
2 garlic cloves
1 bunch fresh parsley
1 small bunch fresh chives
125ml (4fl oz) extra virgin olive oil
1 teaspoon each of cumin and caraway seeds
1.2 litres (2 pints) water
75ml (2½fl oz) balsamic, sherry or red wine vinegar, or to taste
sea salt and black pepper
115g (4oz) plain yoghurt or soured cream

Peel and dice the beetroot, potato, onion and garlic. Chop the parsley fine and the chives into 1cm (½in) lengths.

Sauté the onion in the oil until soft and gently browning, about 8–10 minutes, then add the garlic, cumin and caraway seeds. A few minutes later add the potato and beetroot, and when they are coated in the mixture and well stirred, add the water, bring to the boil and simmer until the beetroot and potato are soft, about 15 minutes.

Use a potato-masher for texture or liquidize for smoothness. Add some vinegar, salt and pepper and the parsley to taste. Serve in bowls with yoghurt or cream, sprinkled with the chives.

beetroot mojitos

Raw and juiced beetroot is full of nutrition and energy. Your first mojito is just for testing to find your own taste, so add salt and/or the lime to taste, then make your proper one for number 2, or 3, or 4.

serves 1
1 small beetroot
1 large sprig mint
¼ teaspoon granulated cane sugar
1 generous slug Cuban rum – preferably 3-year-old
1 pinch sea salt and/or a squeeze of lime

Cut the top and bottom of the beetroot and peel off the skin – you don't want an earthy taste. Cut the beetroot into small cubes, cover with water in a pan and put on a medium heat. Simmer for 10 minutes, strain the liquid off, and leave the liquid to cool, then refrigerate. Discard the beetroot.

Reserve a tiny sprig of the most handsome mint leaves. Crush the remaining mint into the sugar in your chosen glass. Pour in the rum, then the beetroot juice, and add the salt and/or lime juice to taste. Hang the nice mint leaf over the side.

beetroot mojitos with mint

carrots

Carrots as we know them are modern descendants of the wild carrot, an umbel with a white root that grows beside the sea. The familiar orange colour is a result of crossing red and yellow cultivars, and it is still possible to find carrots that are white, yellow, red or purple. The taste is no better in blindfold tests, however, and there is already a strong association between the colour orange and the carroty taste. Differences between varieties are more marked in shape.

growing and harvesting carrots

It is quite common to get two crops out of a season: a young crop of baby carrots in early summer, having been sown in spring; and a late main crop in autumn, having been sown in midsummer. Carrots have very fine seed and the congested cluster of germinated seeds has to be thinned out. This thinning-out alerts the carrot fly to the crop so the idea is to thin out your early carrots before the first generation of carrot fly larvae are about – usually in late May to early June – and to thin out your main-crop carrots after the second generation – in late July and early August. This second thinning-out can wait until it yields baby carrots big enough to eat instead of rooty seedlings.

You can sow carrots successionally, every three or four weeks, starting off the season in pots if the soil is too cold. You can fill the pots with free-draining, sandy soil, which carrots will prefer to stony or heavy clay soil if that is what you have in your garden.

problems with carrots

The top shoulder of carrots gets exposed when the root grows and the rain washes soil away. Sunlight and wind turn it green and coarsen the texture. Although it can be cut off in the kitchen, earthing up lightly with soil will prevent the damage in the first place.

Hot manure and stones can cause carrots to fork and deform in comical ways. Round or short varieties bulk up in a few inches of soil instead of struggling to penetrate heavy clay.

storing carrots

Main-crop carrots can be left in the ground through autumn if slugs are not a problem, but they should be dug up and stored before the frosts, or at least well insulated in situ. Storing (rather than freezing, like other roots) intensifies the flavour and sweetness.

eating and cooking carrots

A handful of baby carrots can be washed and eaten raw over several weeks of a sowing. Early carrots of every type need no peeling or scraping. An inch of leaf stalks can be left on as a handle. Baby carrots can be steamed or boiled whole; larger ones can be cut diagonally first; old winter ones can be roasted with other roots.

carrots with marsala & chervil

This classic Italian dish makes a special fuss of the modest carrot, and quite rightly too.

serves 2

450g (1lb) carrots
100g (3½oz) unsalted butter
1 dessertspoon unrefined sugar
150ml (5 fl oz) Marsala wine
1 small bunch fresh chervil, coriander or
   parsley leaves, chopped

Wash the carrots and cut off the stalks. Cut the carrots diagonally in fat slices.

Put the butter in a thick-bottomed pan with a lid, on a medium heat. When melted, stir in the sugar and let it dissolve. Roll the carrots around to cover them all in melted butter. Pour on the Marsala and put on the lid. Shake the carrots around the pan occasionally to keep them covered and prevent sticking and burning. By the time the Marsala is a buttery sticky glaze, the carrots should be done *al dente*.

Sprinkle a little chopped chervil, coriander or parsley on top and leave the lid on for a minute to soften.

carrot salad

This is a classic Indian salad that is at once refreshing and warming, perfect for a summer day when the sun seems to have gone abroad for a holiday.

serves 4

5 medium carrots
¼ teaspoon cumin seeds
1 pinch mustard seeds
1 small pinch ground cinnamon (optional)
1 dessertspoon extra virgin olive oil
juice of ¼ lemon and ¼ orange
1 small bunch fresh parsley, finely chopped
sea salt and black pepper

Scrub and dry the carrots, there's no need to peel. Shred or grate them coarsely into a serving bowl.

Heat the cumin and mustard seeds for a few minutes in a dry pan, then grind in a pestle and mortar. Add the cinnamon, if using, mix and strew over the carrots. Stir in half the oil and juices, along with the parsley.

Adjust for taste with the other half of the juices, oil and some salt and pepper. Leave the salad to marinate for a while before eating.

carrots with marsala & chervil

new potatoes

Although potatoes have become completely absorbed into our horticulture and cuisine, they were unknown on this side of the Atlantic until their introduction by the Conquistadors in the 16th century. Now they are a staple all around the world and set to become even more popular as traditional staples are ousted to cultivate biofuels.

growing new potatoes

There are literally hundreds of cultivars and selections of potatoes, and it is always worth experimenting by growing several each year. (Just one plant will yield enough for a couple of feasts and where space is at a premium, they can be grown in big tubs or even sturdy bin bags.) When they have been dug fresh from the ground, new potatoes retain the smell of the earth, no matter how cleanly they have been scrubbed. Some experts can tell in what kind of soil they have been grown just from their taste.

digging potatoes

The potato, *Solanum tuberosum*, grows on underground vines. One small seed potato can make a massive network of roots producing pounds of plump tubers and a mass of dense foliage, which eventually bears purple or white flowers similar to those of tomatoes (to which potatoes are closely related). When spuds are grown as a main crop for winter storage, they are only harvested when the top growth has died down, but new potatoes are traditionally harvested when plants begin to flower. Whereas main-crop spuds are lifted from the ground wholesale, dried and stored, new potatoes are eaten freshly dug and if you delve down gently into the soil you can collect a few spuds at a time and leave the rest for another day.

cooking new potatoes

New potatoes are an epicurean delight: it's never about quantity, all about taste. Nothing tastes better than a freshly boiled young potato, sliced and anointed with a lump of butter. It is the sort of taste you can close your eyes and imagine even in the depths of winter. To the memory, taste and smell are the most evocative of all the senses.

Eaten hot or sliced cold to eat with mayonnaise or aïoli and the first of the new crop of salad leaves, new potatoes are always 'of their time', they have the taste of the season, celebrating the first feeling of substantial harvest. Enjoy them at every possible opportunity. Their delicate flavour is easily lost in fussy recipes.

new potato spring stew

So what can you do with two beans, one carrot, a spring onion and half a dozen potatoes? You're not ready to attempt your first DIY 'gargouillou' (an edible display of 40 different vegetables and herbs bought from a French market at 5am, each poached separately and only united by a buttery jus on the plate), but you can make a dish of whatever veg are ready.

serves few or lots
new potatoes
baby root vegetables
beans and peas
summer greens, (see page 114)
to serve
dressing of choice (see page 220) or
    1 tablespoon olive oil plus 15g (½oz) butter
sea salt and black pepper
1 bunch fresh parsley, chopped

Potatoes are best steamed or boiled separately, or rather par-boiled to just not quite done. Baby root vegetables like carrots or turnips steam well and are quicker than potatoes. Beans and peas in pods are a bit quicker than the roots. Either cook each vegetable separately until done and set aside, or, more daringly, start steaming the potatoes. About 8 minutes later put any baby roots into the steamer; about 3 minutes later put in any legumes; about 2 minutes later put in any leaves. Turn them all out about 1 minute later.

Serve like a hot salad with a simple dressing of your choice, or put them into a pan with oil and butter and a tiny pinch of salt. When you can hear sizzling, add about 4 tablespoons of water, put on a lid and give them a shake. Uncover them as the liquid evaporates and coats them all with a sticky sheen, maybe sprinkling on some chopped parsley sparingly.

young roast potatoes

If you are getting lots and lots of young potatoes, this recipe will keep your enthusiasm going as they are irresistible straight out of the oven.

serves 4
1kg (2¼lb) new potatoes
75ml (2½fl oz) olive oil
3 sprigs fresh rosemary, torn into pieces
2 pinches sea salt

Preheat the oven to 200°C/400°F/Gas 6.

Clean the potatoes and steam for about 10 minutes, but before they yield to the point of a sharp knife. Drain and allow the steam to evaporate.

Put the oil and the torn-up sprigs of rosemary into an ovenproof dish and turn the potatoes in the oil. Sprinkle them with salt.

Bake in the preheated oven for about 20–30 minutes. These are best eaten hot out of the oven, all round and glossy, as when they cool down, they go all puckered and a bit acidic.

young roast potatoes

alliums

onions

If any one thing is eaten all over the world, it's onions. Someone somewhere is wiping tears away from their eyes as they cut one up. But we all persevere as it would be unthinkable to cook without them. So why bother? Onions are easy to get hold of because they grow well and you can store them for months. They give both savour and sweetness, depth and body. For harvesting, see page oo.

british onions
These are hard and dense, brown-skinned with white flesh, often with a green tinge, and full of the enzymes that, when released by chopping, create sulphuric acid around your eyes. They grow slowly in tight rings, which helps them store very well for winter use.

spanish onions
These are much sweeter and milder. They grow quickly in warmth and make thick watery rings, which stops them from lasting in storage. Spanish, Dutch and Egyptian onions were cheap to import and this has led to the demand for British onions to have a milder flavour.

yellow onions
Yellow onions, such as 'Walla Walla' can be very sweet, caramelizing and browning for French onion soup, or even baked in their skins. A popular onion with a yellow skin is the Japanese 'Senshyu Yellow' that is actually quite crisp, with a squashed shape (semi-globe) and it stores well. It has a long growing season, being sown through August to September, then over-wintering, then being ready ahead of any rivals in early summer.

red onions
Red onions have had a huge impact in onion circles because they are sweet and mild enough to be eaten raw in salads but spicy enough to make dishes seem 'edgy'. They don't reward being treated like an average white onion as the colour and most of the flavour is lost in slow cooking, and they don't keep as well.

green and pickling onions
Green onions in Britain are largely immature onions with fresh green stalks and undeveloped sulphur enzymes. At this stage they are very similar to spring onions, but spring onions go on to form tight-ringed little bulbs only, not full-size onions. Pickling onions stay dense and crisp after baking, stewing, kebabing and pickling.

'To dry onions fully, lay them out (only one layer deep) on something flat that air can circulate through – a wattle fence panel, wire mesh, slatted wood...or a matrix of sticks.'

Once you harvest your onions they need to be dried. Lay them out on a surface through which air can circulate – here, a fence panel – and allow to dry for a few days.

digging alliums

In spring, your stores of last year's onions, shallots and garlic will be running low or waking up from dormancy and sending up bright green but bitter new shoots. This is when you cast your eyes covetously round the garden at whatever alliums have gone into growth. There is nothing wrong with purloining some of them now; they might be immature but they will be delicious: green garlic, pencil-thin leeks, baby onions, even shallot bulbs can be carefully separated from the cluster early.

when to harvest alliums

Your main crop for storing through the year will benefit from having plenty of sunshine for ripening. Although you want juicy bulbs, slopping on too much water is counterproductive. Let the bulbs draw moisture up from normally moist soil at their own rate. Ideally, the leaves of onions, garlic and shallots wither in a good summer and the energy and goodness of the leaves is channelled into the swelling bulbs.

With onions, rot usually begins at the neck. Impatient gardeners or those threatened by heavy rain or floods at harvest time, hurry along the ripening and drying process by flattening the stalks of their onions. If you can let the onion do this for itself as part of the maturing cycle, you won't bruise and tear the fibres of the stalks at the neck, especially if there is still green tissue and water in them. Onions with sun-dried necks will string up and store better.

how to harvest alliums

Using a small fork, loosen the soil to one side of the bulbs you are lifting and pull out gently by the leaves. If you might rip them, dig more and lift by the bulb. Shake off any loose soil.

drying and storing alliums

To dry onions fully, lay them out (only one layer deep) on something flat that air can circulate through – a wattle fence panel, wire mesh, slatted wood or a matrix of sticks. Let them

Loosen the soil around the base with a small garden fork, then pull the allium out by its leaves. If it doesn't come out easily, dig more and try again.

Shake off the loose soil and separate the bulbs if the type of allium requires this (here, red spring onions).

sunbathe, turning occasionally for a few days or until the leaves are shrivelled and the bulbs feel dry. Cover them up immediately if there is to be rain. Plait the leaves or tear them off providing they are completely desiccated and store in a net, suspended, so air can circulate.

To dry and store soft-neck garlic, treat like onions. For hard-neck garlic, tie the stalks together loosely and suspend a bunch of them, or, cut through the vertical stem a few inches above the bulb and store in a net or on a rack. Shallots can have the clusters broken up and the bulbs stored in a net or spread on a rack. All alliums should be stored out of sunlight somewhere cool, dry and airy.

Shallots grow in clusters of bulbs – harvest the whole cluster at once and break into individual bulbs before storing.

potato & onion rösti

The aroma of potato and onion rösti frying is very appetizing, drawing on memories of chip shops and fairground stalls.

serves 2
2 large waxy potatoes
1 large sweet onion
sea salt and black pepper
2 tablespoons olive oil
100g (3½oz) unsalted butter

Peel the potatoes and onion. Grate the potato on a coarse grater into a large bowl of warm water. Swill it around to rinse out any starch. Dry the potato in a clean tea-towel. Cut the onion into thin rings and mix together with the potato, and some salt and pepper.

In a frying pan, heat the oil and when it is hot, drop in the butter and the potato mixture, flattening it down with a spatula or fish-slice. After a few minutes, check the underneath, and if it is browning, flip the rösti over, pressing it down again. Repeat this process, trying a bit of the least-done inner potato for tenderness.

caramelized onion jam

Onions are obviously the foundation for very many dishes. A tight crisp onion is a good friend when you find it a long time from last year's cropping season. Damaged onions or onions that won't store well because of poor ripening weather can be used en masse in things like onion soup, or roasted and caramelized.

makes 1 small pot
4 or 5 large onions
100g (3½oz) unsalted butter
1 tablespoon unrefined sugar
125ml (4fl oz) red wine or sherry vinegar
   or both
300ml (10fl oz) red wine
3 sprigs fresh thyme
sea salt and black pepper

Peel and slice the onions thinly.

Melt the butter in a heavy pan and soften the onion for about 10 minutes. Add the sugar and dissolve it thoroughly. When it is bubbling, add the liquids, herbs and some seasoning.

Let it simmer away in the pan on top of the hob, uncovered, until it is thick and syrupy, a good 30–45 minutes.

radishes & bread with caramelized onion jam

98

shallots

If raw onion blows your head off, and even spring onions are too powerful in a salad, you need an introduction to shallots. They are refined, sophisticated and full of savoir-faire. No wonder they have always been habitués of top-flight Parisian kitchens.

growing shallots

Shallots are small bulbs that grow in a cluster and usually look like small-scale elongated onions. They have much less enzyme in their membranes than onions and generally lack that full-on flavour. Their flavour is more complex and subtle as they have more flavonoids and phenols than onions. What they do have is a light, slightly sour and tangy taste and a dense but tender texture.

The final size of shallots is partly determined by the space in which they have to grow. Too tightly packed in and the bulbs will be very difficult to peel. Too widely spaced and the bulbs will resemble small onions. For harvesting, see page oo.

preparing and cooking shallots

Thin growth rings mean that with a sharp knife it is possible to cut them up very finely; in fact you can mince them. This allows you then to distribute the tiny pieces right the way through a sauce or dressing. There are no concentrations or lumps of shallot to unbalance the flavours or change the texture.

If you find that the miniature-onion types of shallot are too robust and oniony, they can be blanched in boiling water to dissolve their sulphurousness or poached in milk if they are for a sauce béarnaise or similar.

french shallots

These have grey skins and are called 'griselle', or *Allium oschaninii*. This is the gourmet shallot, 'Echalote Grise'. Most shallots that are available to the home-grower are *Allium cepa var. aggregatum* (or multiplier onions). They were confusingly once called *Allium ascalonicum* and hence called 'scallions', which is also sometimes applied to either onions that are immature and green, or to spring onions. Even if your harvest 'only' resembles small cigar- or globe-shaped mini-onions, they will be extremely useful in summer cooking.

asian shallots

Asian varieties of shallot have red skins and purplish or red flushes to the flesh.

other types of shallot

There are now many shallot varieties bred from Dutch types that resemble miniature onions, mainly in a globe shape, some flesh tinged with purple or green. They are derived from commercial varieties as they are tough and solid enough to resist handling damage, keep well or have big yields. A new variety is the 'banana shallot' or 'Echalion', which is a cross between a shallot and an onion and of a size between the two, with only the good features of both parents, mild but easy-peeling, according to its breeders.

shallot dressing

Shallots are like sophisticated miniature onions, tighter and more minceable, with much less sulphur. This makes them more suitable than onions for small-scale dishes requiring more subtlety. You can use them raw in dressing, which you couldn't even do with spring onions.

serves 4
4 shallots
150ml (5fl oz) white wine
1 bay leaf
2 green peppercorns
sea salt and black pepper
2 tablespoons extra virgin olive oil

Peel the shallots and cut in half vertically. Lay them cut-side down and slice them across into semi-circles as thinly as you can.

Put the wine in a pan with the bay leaf and add the peppercorns after bruising or crushing them. Bring to the boil and immediately turn off the heat. Put in the shallot, working it round to blanch for 2 minutes.

Take out the shallot, using a slotted spoon, letting the wine drain off. This blanched shallot, seasoned, can now be used in a salad or as a garnish.

When the wine has cooled, whisk the olive oil into the liquid and use as a dressing.

roast balsamic shallots

Roasting shallots brings out their sweetness, without losing their full flavour. Their cute size makes them very tempting, all sticky and glistening.

serves 4–6
20–30 shallots
150ml (5fl oz) extra virgin olive oil
sea salt and black pepper
balsamic vinegar

Preheat the oven to 180°C/350°F/Gas 4.

Peel the shallots and cut them in half.

Warm the oil up in a large ovenproof dish that can take them all without burying any. Plonk the shallots in the dish and give them a good sprinkle of salt and pepper. Roll and shake the dish to cover every shallot in a coating of oil. Brush or sprinkle on extra oil if you can't cover them all. Shake and sprinkle a good few drops of vinegar (about 2 tablespoons) over them.

Bake in the preheated oven, turning them round after 10 minutes. After about another 10 minutes they should be glossy brown, beginning to char outside and tender inside.

roast balsamic shallots

VARIETIES

HARD-NECKED 'LAUTREC WIGHT' and 'PURPLE MOLDOVAN' grow well with a full flavour.

SOFT-NECKED 'SOLENT WIGHT' and 'MEDITERRANEAN WIGHT' grow well in Britain. 'CRISTO' has a long dormancy so will store until spring.

garlic

A little bulb with a huge impact, garlic magnifies itself leaving a trail everywhere it goes, on your fingers, in your cooking, on your breath. But it doesn't just announce itself, it changes all ingredients it encounters.

growing garlic

Garlic is usually easy to grow. One of the single cloves that makes up the bulb, in a tight ring with five to a dozen others, will go on to produce a new shoot, then a new flowering stem and its own cluster of cloves, unless you eat it first. Garlic can appreciate cool growing conditions, not just Mediterranean ones, and the original species may have been Siberian. Wild garlic has no trouble growing around British woodlands, but bulbs imported for eating may be an unsuitable variety for growing in your garden.

different types of garlic

Garlic varieties have been bred that don't store very long but suit the local growing conditions. They can be among the very best flavoured of all. Some are called 'hard-necked' because they die back after the growing season, the shrivelled leaves surrounding a rigid flower stem. You can store them for three or so months before they shrink and soften. 'Soft-necked' varieties have no such stiff flower stem and the shrivelled leaves are soft and floppy and can be plaited into a string of bulbs.

eating garlic

All parts of garlic are edible: the cloves, the flowering stem known as the scape and the collection of bulbils that make up the flower head. 'Purple Moldovan' has edible 'rocamboles', or twirls, up the flower stem. When garlic grows in late spring, its fresh green shoots are eminently edible and the clove can be extracted from the thick covering of leaf layers around it. This is 'green garlic', mild but full of garlic memories. You can eat this raw, the leaves shredded or wilted into salads. 'Mediterranean Wight' is especially good green. You can pull out or cut off the scape and eat it like chives if it is a 'soft-neck' or blanch it for a minute for a succulent, munchy garnish if it is a 'hard-neck'. This can encourage the cloves to fatten up a bit more.

chopping, slicing and cooking garlic

Garlic cloves have the densest concentration of fibres of any vegetable. This makes them very easy to slice if the knife is sharp. Violent bruising releases more flavour and separates the skin easily. An enzyme allinaise oxidizes in contact with air, so cut garlic should not be stored and dishes should be eaten with the garlic freshly introduced, ideally. The hot and sharp taste of raw garlic is mollified by cooking as the heat destroys the allicin that causes it. Burning garlic during cooking makes it bitter. Cloves that have been stored a long time and are coming out of dormancy may have a green shoot coming out of the centre and removing this will avoid bitterness too.

roast garlic

The smell of garlic cooking makes every dish it is in irresistibly delicious. It is the magic ingredient that elevates all the run-of-the-mill neighbours and realizes their potential. It is tempting and very healthy to eat it raw, but it's usually too overpowering. Roasting it is at the other extreme, where the acrid omnipresence is replaced by a sweet depth of flavour.

serves 4

3 heads garlic (about 30 cloves)
150ml (5fl oz) extra virgin olive oil
2 bay leaves
1 sprig fresh rosemary
5 fresh sage leaves
3 sprigs fresh thyme
sea salt and black pepper

Preheat the oven to 170°C/325°F/Gas 3.

Separate the garlic cloves and cut off the hard bases.

Warm the oil in a large ovenproof tray and stir everything else in.

When all the cloves are oily and the herbs are spread through, roast in the moderate oven for 20–30 minutes. Keep checking on them, stirring them round so they do not burn, adding water to the tray if necessary.

Save some when they are semi-soft for a daring side dish, say with almonds or good olives. Carry on cooking the rest until they are soft inside. Take them out of the oil, which you can save for cooking later.

Squeeze the soft flesh out of the skins by hand or with a spoon. The garlic purée is useful for many dips and dressings, and especially for mashed potatoes and the soup, (see right).

garlic soup

If you use some roast garlic purée or oil, this recipe is not as full-on as it sounds, but is satisfyingly delicious. The bread should be very dry, preferably ciabatta-style. As the egg is barely cooked, it must be very fresh.

serves 2

1 shallot
1 mild but piquant chilli pepper
olive oil (perhaps some of the roast garlic oil)
1 tablespoon oily roast garlic purée (see left)
1 handful young spinach leaves, chopped into strips
600ml (1 pint) hot water
sea salt and black pepper
about 2 thick slices stale bread
1 small free-range organic egg (optional)

Peel and mince the shallot and mince the chilli. In a pan sauté them gently in some oil for about 6 minutes. When they are soft, add the garlic purée, and when that is hot, add the spinach and the water. Simmer for 8–10 minutes. Season to taste.

For serving, grill or toast the bread with some oil, or tear lumps into the bottom of the dishes. If using, whisk the egg and stir slowly round the soup pan to cook the egg stracciatella-style.

garlic soup

leaves & salad

spinach

Spinach is all about green – the freshest, greenest green veg, the tenderest leaf, and the green in sauce vert and green pasta. It is a crop you have to keep sowing because it is short-lived; it is also temperamental but you can overtake failures by keeping on top of it. It is also very delectable and useful, but it is prone to self-exaggeration, as a massive armful cooks down to only a quarter-of-a-panful.

growing spinach

Spinach thrives with plenty of moisture and fertility at its roots and needs to grow quickly. Baby leaves can be taken for eating raw, but this can slow the plant down for making big cooking leaves later on. Spinach bolts easily, but the leaves on a flowering stem of a variety like 'Spinacio Viridis' can be picked and used perfectly well. You have to catch the stem early, and the plant will now redouble its efforts to flower, so you have to keep on top of it, mindful that its days are numbered.

preparing spinach

Grit and soil seem to be disproportionately troublesome with spinach and patient washing and soaking is worth the time spent.

cooking spinach

The vitality and colour of spinach is very fragile, it can be overcooked into a dark green slime. Traditionally, spinach leaves would be stripped from the stalks and boiled in a little water. The leaves collapse and shrink into a homogenous blob surrounded by dark, almost dyed, water. Attempts to drain the spinach end up with it getting squeezed in a colander. It still seems sopping wet but with an acidic teeth-grating mineral flavour. If you tear it roughly and steam it over fast-boiling salted water with a squeeze of lemon juice, it cooks to tender very quickly, and provided it doesn't have to sit around before serving, the bright, luminescent green is saved and there is almost no excess water. There is none of the after-taste and the nutrients aren't tipped down the sink.

a substitute for spinach

An excellent substitute for spinach is 'spinach beet', aka leaf beet, aka perpetual spinach. This is a hardy and reliable plant that has no intention of bolting, and even if it flowers in its second year, leaves can still be picked. Perpetual spinach has a thicker, tougher leaf, and a delicious but discardable stem – it just takes a tiny bit more cooking than spinach. Even the babiest leaves work well in a raw salad.

'Timing is everything,
as spinach sown too
early in spring will
bolt, yet seed sown
in hot weather often
doesn't germinate.'

picking spinach

A vigorous chard plant or a patch of spinach in your garden is like having your own always-open store. When you want a fresh green vegetable for a meal, you just go out and pick it. You pick what you need when you need it; you don't have to clear a crop from the ground.

When leafy vegetables are in a growing phase, as in spring and early summer, they are increasing the size of their leaves and throwing up more all the time. Picking a few at a time doesn't really set them back at all. Sometimes it just encourages them to make more. In the normal run of things, leafy plants will want to make flowers and seeds and this can involve putting up a central stem as tall as possible, like with chard, or many stems as with spinach. Either way, this process hijacks most of the plant's energy and can lead to the deterioration of the leaves.

lettuce and spinach

LETTUCE is the worst example, when it 'bolts' and runs to seed, as the leaves, which the last time you picked them were sweet and delicious, are now bitter and inedible. If you keep picking baby leaves from the centre of the plant, you will be pinching out the baby flower stems at

You should harvest spinach on a regular basis to encourage further leaf production. Remove flower stems as they appear, as these will zap the plant's energy.

Pick leaves from the base of the stalk, and make sure you harvest both the tough outer leaves to keep the plant young and the inner succulent leaves, perfect for salads.

the same time. This only buys you time though, because the plant will try even harder now to throw up a flower stem. You just have to keep thwarting it, until the plant exhausts itself. **SPINACH** must be picked regularly for this reason, and the baby leaves from the centre are thin and soft enough to eat raw in a salad. Big side leaves should also be picked to keep the plant young. The stalk is very tender when cooked but has a less smooth texture in the mouth and should still be picked but discarded if you don't want it in your recipe.

other salad leaves

MIZUNA, ROCKET AND MUSTARD are easily picked by squeezing the stem between your thumb-nail and your forefinger. You can pick out the best young leaves for eating and the tired old ones can be picked off to clean up the plant. Large and bolted mizuna leaves can be steamed or wilted, as can pak-choi even if it has stretched tall for flowering.

spinach beet, kale and chard

PERPETUAL OR 'SPINACH BEET' can be cropped hard all through the year, any baby leaves picked out for raw salads, tougher leaves for cooking. **KALE** can have the big outer leaves ripped off first, in a downward motion, if they are in good condition, otherwise keep harvesting the inner leaves. Despite the very substantial ribbed-stalks of chard, outer leaves can be ripped off unless it is tearing the stalk away messily, in which case the stalks cut easily with a sharp knife.

steamed spinach

Spinach is still revered despite the fact that everybody now knows it was accidentally credited with ten times more nutrition than it really has – and nobody actually wants to look like Popeye anyway! On cooking, it shrinks to a tenth of its original bulk so the equilibrium of the universe is restored.

serves 2

4 large handfuls spinach leaves
1 garlic clove
1 thumb-sized piece fresh root ginger
1 dessertspoon vegetable oil (groundnut ideally)

Wash the spinach leaves and tear any enormous ones in half. Peel and slice the garlic very finely. Cut the skin off the ginger and cut into flakes similar in size to the garlic.

Heat the oil in a wok and when it starts smoking, tip in the garlic and ginger.

Agitate the wok, and before the garlic goes brown, throw in the spinach. Push it down into the wok to stop the garlic burning, and roll it around.

When the spinach is hot and covered in oily garlic and ginger, it is done, about 30 seconds.

saag aloo

Curries don't have to be determined by shop-bought sauces. This one is fresh and bright.

serves 2

450g (1lb) waxy potatoes
1 carrot
1 onion or shallot
1 small fresh red chilli pepper
1 thumb-sized piece fresh root ginger
1 large garlic clove
2 large handfuls spinach leaves
½ teaspoon each of black onion, mustard and cumin seeds
¼ teaspoon turmeric powder (optional)
½ tablespoon thin vegetable oil, but olive will do
125ml (4fl oz) water

Wash the potatoes or peel if they are disfigured. Steam or boil until they are tender, about 15–20 minutes. Peel and cut the carrot into small chunks. Add these to the potatoes for the last 10 minutes of their cooking time, then drain.

Peel and finely dice the onion. Finely chop the chilli, and peel and finely chop the ginger. Smash and peel the garlic. Wash the spinach leaves and tear any enormous ones in half.

Using a large pan with a lid, fry the spices in the oil. When they pop violently, tip in the onion, chilli and ginger and stir around to cool the spices and start their cooking, lid on. After 5 minutes, add the garlic, and when it's gone quite translucent, add the water, lid back on, to make more of a sauce.

Roll the potatoes around in the mixture, then stir in the spinach and turn the heat off. The residual heat is enough to wilt the tender spinach leaves and keep them bright green. The curry is now ready to be served.

saag aloo

summer greens

Many of the leaves that introduce themselves tentatively in spring are abundant in summer. Instead of one or two tiny leaves plucked from here and there to make up a motley collection, great handfuls of one kind are suddenly possible.

Unfortunately the heat of summer makes salad-leaf crops accelerate, and sunburn and water-stress will make them flower and run to seed. Even if you pick new leaves and flowering stems daily, the plants will tire themselves out. But new plants will establish quickly, even from seed, and you will soon be harvesting salads again.

spinach and beetroot leaves
Spinach is the archetypal summer sprinter and you must crop it with a vengeance. Beetroot leaves can be confiscated for salads or wilting, and perpetual spinach must not be neglected. Leaves will double in size within a week.

lettuces
Open-heart (aka loose-hearted, loose-leafed and cut-and-come-again) lettuces offer a light cropping all year round with successional sowing, and should not be neglected now. But the other lettuce types – the less hardy crisphead and cos especially can be enjoyed as one-off crops and eaten intensively! Cos lettuces can be cooked, as in several French recipes, because they can have tight hearts, flavour and texture.

mizuna, rocket and other leaves
Mizuna, mibuna and rocket increase the number of their leaves and in the course of the summer there is a coarsening of the texture. Large mizuna leaves that are too much to eat in a salad can be wilted after taking off the stalks. Wild rocket lags behind the cultivated one in growth so it can find its way into more salads in high summer.

mustard greens
Mustard greens, *Brassica juncea*, are seldom green, and varieties with a purple tinge to the leaves are well-flavoured with a hot, mustard taste but also a fuller mellowness. The leaves are large; they make a good bed for something else if they are shredded into 5mm (¼in) strips across the leaf. A good handful can be wilted with a mashed clove of garlic, a big pinch of smoked paprika powder and a splash of red wine vinegar.

pak-choi
Pak-choi is a very speedy crop – a July sowing might be edible in August. It is a 'long and thin' crop in autumn, winter and spring, but in summer it can be 'fast and fat', and whole plants can be uprooted for their crisp white bases and quickly steamed or braised.

braised lettuce

The French have a tradition of cooking lettuce, which we have lost. A few little hearts are a nice addition to a dish of peas. They are surprisingly tasty and substantial cooked like this.

serves 2

3 or 4 small lettuce hearts (little gem type)
1 shallot, peeled
55g (2oz) butter or 1 tablespoon olive oil
1 teaspoon mild miso paste
300ml (10fl oz) hot water

Wash the lettuce hearts but leave whole.

Dice the shallot finely and stew gently in the butter or oil in a pan with a lid. Do not let it fry or brown.

Dissolve the miso paste in the hot water. Add this along with the hearts to the shallot pan and simmer gently with the lid on for about 4 minutes, agitating the hearts and adding more water as necessary.

The hearts should be on the soft side of munchy, with plenty of liquor around them.

dressed salad leaves

'Cut-and-come-again' type salad leaves benefit from a daily pick-over so if you are thinning out the damaged or ugly leaves, they are never too bad. Otherwise pick a selection of whatever individual leaves catch your eye and take your fancy.

serves 2

1 large handful mixed young salad leaves – for example, mâche (corn salad), mesclun (baby lettuce, cress, rocket, chervil et al), mizuna, baby pak-choi – plus edible flowers such as nasurtium, pot marigold and borage

dressing

1 teaspoon cane sugar
1 piled teaspoon wholegrain mustard
sea salt and black pepper
2 teaspoons balsamic vinegar
white wine vinegar, to taste
7–8 tablespoons extra virgin olive oil

In an empty jam jar mix the sugar, mustard and a little salt and pepper together, then add the vinegars – a little of the white wine vinegar at first; you can always add more later. Pour in the oil, put the lid on firmly and shake the jar so you have a mixed-up emulsion. Taste and add more white wine vinegar if you wish to. Shake again.

Wait a minute for the dressing on the underside of the lid to drop back into the jar unless you want to be licking your fingers. Usually it is too unctuous so add dribbles of wine vinegar to get the balance to taste.

Dress the leaves and toss just before you serve and eat.

dressed salad leaves

VARIETIES

ROUND 'RAPID RED SANOVA', 'ROSSO GIGANTE'.

LONG 'FLAMBOYANT', 'CANDELO DI FUOCO'.

MOOLI 'BIRRA DI MONACO', 'CANDELO DI GHIACCIO'.

radishes

The traditional English salad is as bad an advertisement for radishes as you can imagine – coarse peppery pink bombs with a brassicacious after-burp. However, there are optimum ways of growing radishes and a wide range of types available.

Radishes (*Raphanus sativus*) are from the mustard family and they have been bred and selected for many years all over Asia and Europe. Consequently there are a huge number of variations of form, colour, texture and size: round and oval; green, white, pink, purple and bi-colour; crisp and dense; marble-sized to skinny marrow-sized mooli.

growing radishes

Radishes are universally popular because they grow so well. In fact, they are easier to grow than they are to eat. You can be eating full-grown radishes within three weeks of sowing them. Firstly, germination is very reliable. Best sown in situ on to warming earth in spring, they can be sprinkled thinly in rows or scattered carelessly in a wide patch. They will grow well even if congested together or they will happily root a hand's width all round away from their neighbours. A spare few inches of soil between planted vegetables or on empty space between crops make them a handy catch-crop.

If you have the taste for them, they can be sown late-February to early-August for successional cropping.

harvesting radishes

You can watch the radish shoulders growing on the surface of the soil as their taproots penetrate the soil. Keep them well watered. At an early stage you can harvest most of the leaves – baby ones raw in salads, small ones shredded for a peppery lift to mild salads, and bigger ones wilted as a green vegetable, akin to beet leaves or coarse coriander or celery leaves in the Asian giants. Ease radishes out of the soil with the help of a small fork when they reach a good size for eating and use them straightaway so they don't dry out.

eating young radishes

Fresh, young radishes are mild flavoured, crisp and succulent. One delight of a prime raw radish is that its texture lends itself to very accurate slicing. A sharp knife and a steady hand can produce paper-thin translucent rounds. Some more exotic radishes have multicoloured markings throughout the flesh like a stick of rock.

eating asian radishes

Asian radishes, especially Japanese mooli or daikon, give a great kick to other raw root vegetables. Shred radishes, beetroot, carrots and celeriac together in fine juliennes and drench in a robust dressing, even slicing on the green tops of salad onions.

eating mature radishes

Over-mature radishes feel spongy and the delicate spiciness of youth becomes strongly peppery and then indigestibly manky. Experiments in cooking beyond the swiftest of blanchings are inedible and bitter. Far better to keep a rapid turnaround in sowing and cropping and only eat them crisp and young.

radish & fennel salad

This is quite an intense salad as the peppery taste of the radish is augmented by the aniseed taste of the fennel, and both are extremely crunchy.

serves 2

1 shallot
juice and finely grated zest of 1 lemon
1 handful radishes
1 large or 2 small fennel bulbs
1 dessertspoon extra virgin olive oil
sea salt and black pepper
1 handful mustard greens

Either use the shallot from the shallot dressing recipe (see page 102), or peel and thinly slice the shallot (about 3mm/⅛in, or whatever is practical because the shallot, radish and fennel should be sliced the same thickness). Let the shallot marinate in the zest and juice of the lemon for half an hour.

Slice the radishes thinly; quarter the fennel and slice thinly too. Add these to the marinating shallot. Stir them round with the olive oil and some salt and pepper.

Shred the mustard greens diagonally into quite large pieces and spread on a serving plate. Pile the sliced salad on top to serve.

radish & rocket salad

People either love or hate radishes. For us, small baby salad radishes are a lightweight food eaten raw, a real signpost of summer days.

serves 2

1 handful radishes
2 handfuls rocket leaves
1 shallot
1 large ripe tomato (optional)
1 tablespoon extra virgin olive oil
juice of ½ large lemon
sea salt and black pepper

Slice the radishes into 3mm (⅛in) discs or semi-circles. Wash and dry the rocket and tear in half. Peel and cut the shallot into thin slices. Cut the tomato into quarters and slice about 1cm (½in) thick across, if using.

Toss in the oil and lemon juice, with salt and pepper to taste.

radish & rocket salad

VARIETIES

Pickling varieties were selected for preserving in vinegar because they could never mature in time in northern climates and their small size was an asset in the pickle jar.

'PARISIAN PICKLING' grows well outside and you can crop baby 5cm (2in) **'CORNICHONS'**, next size up 10cm (4in) gherkins, or 15–20cm (6–8in) normal-sized cucumbers.

Another general purpose pickling and slicing cucumber is **'WAUTOMA'**, specially bred to resist all the likely cucumber diseases and is reliable and prolific. It is suitable for indoors or outdoors, up a support or on the floor. It does have tiny white spines but they wipe off easily.

cucumber

There are plenty of confusing facts and half-remembered myths about growing cucumbers but you can successfully keep it simple. You can grow cucumbers in Britain just as well outdoors as indoors unless the summer is a complete wash-out. Traditionally, outdoor cucumbers were called ridge cucumbers and they were expected to have quite tough thick skins, even though some had very thin skins and some were more like melons. Nowadays, outdoor cucumbers have soft skins and are not at all bitter until the seeds inside are very well developed.

growing cucumbers

Pinching out male flowers and white-washing the greenhouse glass are arcane practices that don't need to concern the grow-your-own gardener. Although cucumbers are thought of as summer sun-lovers, they appreciate a bit of shade around the middle of the day because their leaves are quite thin.

Above all, cucumbers like to grow smoothly without interruption so sow them in a pot, harden them off for a week outside and then plant out in a sheltered, sunny, well-drained spot in the garden. If you have space there are scrambling bush varieties but growing cucumbers up a trellis or bamboo wigwam or frame allows the fruits to hang down and you are more likely to spot them.

Water normally until the fruits are beginning to set, then make sure they never want for water. Mid-season they will appreciate a diluted seaweed or tomato feed.

picking cucumbers

Freshly picked cucumbers are crisp and full of water. If you pick them from the bottom up, more will form higher up and, by continuously picking young fruits before the seeds inside get a chance to ripen, the plant will keep producing cucumbers. You only need to eat fresh young fruits, not seedy old yellowing ones.

cooking cucumbers

With so many cucumbers, from say two or three plants, you might try cooking some: peel, deseed and cut into 1cm (½in) chunks, then gently sauté in pale butter with some mild herbs like chervil or dill until just tender.

pickling cucumbers

Small pickling cucumbers can served with shallots, herbs and wine vinegar after salting and draining them for an hour. Pickling in jars with boiled vinegar, herbs and spices is an easy way of keeping them going into winter.

cucumber raita

Even when you pick a cucumber in a scorching hot greenhouse, it is still the epitome of cool. This raita is a lovely foil to anything fiery, such as a curry, or a salve for afterwards.

serves 2–4
1 teaspoon fresh cumin seeds
1 cucumber
225g (8oz) plain yoghurt
sea salt and black pepper

Heat the cumin seeds in a dry pan for about 1 minute, but stop immediately if they start to smoke or burn. They carry on cooking even off the heat. Grind them in a pestle and mortar.

Top and tail the cucumber. Using a sharp knife or peeler, take off the skin in long strips. Cut the cucumber lengthways in quarters and take out any big seeds. Cut the cucumber across in very thin slices.

Mix the cumin into the yoghurt in a bowl and stir in the cucumber, trying to separate the slices and cover all of them with yoghurt. Season to taste with salt and pepper and serve immediately.

cucumber raita

green gazpacho

Even though you aren't a farm labourer toiling under a merciless Spanish sun, you can still self-righteously enjoy gazpacho when you have grown all the vegetables yourself and have your very own blisters and sunburn to prove it.

serves 4
2 medium garlic cloves
2 small shallots
2 tablespoons extra virgin olive oil
2 medium cucumbers
1 green pepper (optional)
1 green chilli (optional)
2 handfuls spinach leaves (or perpetual spinach)
leaves from 1 bunch fresh parsley
600ml (1 pint) cold water
2 tablespoons ground almonds (optional)
3 pinches sea salt, or to taste

Smash the garlic and remove the skins. Peel and finely chop the shallots. Gently stew the garlic and shallot in the olive oil for about 8 minutes to soften them without burning or frying. Keep a lid on the pan and add a little extra water if there is any danger of browning.

Meanwhile, lightly peel the cucumbers and cut them into quarters lengthways. Cut away the seeds if they are too big or there are too many of them. Cut them into 2cm (¾in) dice. Skin and deseed the pepper and chilli, if using, and cut into similar small dice. Add them to the pan with the cucumber and stew gently for 10 minutes or until the cucumber is a little soft.

Take the pan off the heat and stir in the green leaves and the parsley to wilt them. Tip into a blender with the water and the almonds, if using, and liquidize, or mash and whisk by hand. Add salt to taste and more water if the soup is too thick. Serve warm or cold.

VARIETIES

Famous cherry tomatoes are 'GARDENER'S DELIGHT' and 'SUNGOLD'.

Good beefsteak tomatoes include 'COSTOLUTO FIORENTINO' and 'COSTOLUTO GENOVESE'.

'AMISH PASTE' is a giant plum tomato perfect for cooking down.

tomatoes

To be able to eat fragrant tomatoes ripened in your own garden and warmed by the summer sun is one of the main reasons for many people to grow their own. There are hundreds of tomato varieties, bred for different characteristics. In an ideal world the home-grower would know what kind of tomato they wanted and choose accordingly.

the main types of tomatoes

The two main types are bush tomatoes, that make compact plants, and vine tomatoes, which try to grow as long as possible. Bush tomatoes fruit under the discretion of the plant itself, which decides how much of a crop the shoots can support. Fruits ripen earlier with less trouble than with vine tomatoes but the yield is smaller. Vine tomatoes need help to grow in the right direction and for the gardener to pinch out side-shoots that might distract it from its journey.

Plants of both types have been bred specifically for growing indoors (under glass or plastic) or outdoors, and some types will do in either place. Vine types need tying into supports; most others require some sort of staking to support fruiting trusses, which can get quite heavy.

eating raw salad tomatoes

Salad tomatoes should have a thin skin and sugars should already be present to balance out the acidity of the juice. All the flavours should be available in the first mouthful. Cherry tomatoes, usually hanging in long trusses on vine tomatoes, are ideal for eating raw. The yellow and orange ones usually ripen earlier in the season. Traditional slicing tomatoes for salads, like 'Ailsa Craig', were displaced by industrial pap like 'Moneymaker', but now good Italian beefsteak tomatoes are available.

cooking with tomatoes

Cooking tomatoes still need to be a bit sweet, but too much can make sophisticated recipes taste childish. And they don't want to be too watery, but firm-fleshed to resist disintegration. On the other hand, most industrial tomatoes have neither sweetness nor flavour, so Godfather-style tomato sauces need to have sugar added. Almost all industrial tomatoes, even 'vine-ripened', are grown hydroponically under glass, in gutters of running water, and liquid fertilizers are added to a timetable. As yet, there is no additive for flavour.

peeling tomatoes

To peel thick-skinned tomatoes for a salad or for sauces, snick a tiny cut into the skin and drop them into a bowl of boiling water for 15–20 seconds. Scoop them out and ideally plunge them into another bowl of very cold water or wait for them to cool enough to handle. The snick should have opened out and the skin should peel away.

tomato, mozzarella, avocado & fennel salad

Tomatoes that have been left to mature on the vine will have become much sweeter than commercial hydroponic tomatoes. These sugars inside help hugely to counterbalance the sour acidity of most varieties. This dish resembles an edible Italian flag.

serves 4
2 large handfuls baby rocket leaves
3 large ripe tomatoes
2 large mozzarella balls
1 large or 2 small ripe avocados
1 large fennel bulb or 3 small bulblets
dressing of choice (see page 220)

Cover a large plate with the rocket leaves. Slice the tomatoes and the mozzarella and arrange on top of the rocket in separate stripes.

Cut the avocado in half from top to bottom around the stone. Twist the two halves away from each other and pull apart. Impale the stone that has been left in one of the halves with the point of a sharp knife and lever it out. With a sharp spoon, slice out the avocado and arrange in stripes on the other side of the mozzarella. Shave over the fennel and dress generously.

chunky tomato sauce

This recipe takes a wet tomato sauce that can be reduced to a sticky flavourful paste that can be spread on toast or grilled with cheese.

makes a lot of sauce or a little paste
2 large onions
3 large carrots
3 celery stalks
½ fennel bulb (optional)
125ml (4fl oz) extra virgin olive oil
6–8 garlic cloves
3 bay leaves
1 bunch fresh parsley
1.3–1.8kg (3–4lb) very ripe, even split, tomatoes
sea salt and black pepper and sugar, to taste
half a dozen fresh basil and marjoram leaves

Peel and trim the onions, carrots, celery and fennel, if using, as appropriate, then chop up. Sauté in the oil in a large pan for 5 minutes. Peel and smash the garlic and add to the pan with the bay leaves and cook until the garlic just begins to turn colour. Tip in the parsley and the tomatoes, both roughly chopped.

Let the sauce simmer for 10–20 minutes, stirring frequently. Adjust the seasoning, adding the remaining chopped herbs and using sugar to taste. At this stage, you can take out some for a sauce and carry on simmering the remainder to concentrate it for keeping.

Use a blender or push the sauce through the holes of a colander with a wooden spoon. Transfer it to another saucepan and reduce for 20 minutes. Then put it in an ovenproof dish with a lid. This can be left in a low oven for several hours, or in a very low oven overnight.

chunky tomato sauce

summer herbs

By summer, bathed in warm sunshine, vegetables are starting to develop their full flavour. The herbs we use to intensify that flavour in cooking are poised to embellish them, bursting with aroma, rich and redolent of the Mediterranean.

borage Borage (see top left) is a coarse-looking herb and it seeds itself uninvited, but it is always welcome because bees love it – they will pollinate your courgettes and runner beans when they visit.

oregano/ marjoram Oregano (see top right) is marjoram. It is native to the UK, growing on sunny banks in dry soils. The hotter it gets, the more oils are released from tiny glands on the back of its leaves and the more flavoursome it becomes. There are many different forms, selections and cultivars. My favourite was from our neighbours and has variegated leaves.

Pick oregano fresh, pulling leaves off the stems or freeze whole stems and crumble leaves later straight from the freezer.

basil Basil (see bottom left) epitomizes the perfume of summer herbs. A tender annual, it needs to be started off from seed early, sown in February if you have a greenhouse or a spare warm windowsill. Make sure seed is fresh; if you allow one plant to flower each year, you can collect your own seed for the next year. Basil needs lots of water. In common with mint, it needs fertile soil too, with plenty of nitrogen, so humus is important. In the garden it should not be planted out until all danger of frost is past.

Often basil is grown in pots or reclaimed containers – old olive-oil cans have become emblematic – but whatever you use make sure there is good drainage and rich compost.

The large-leaved or 'Italian' basil that most of us grow is by no means the only variety. There is a 'Greek' basil with very small leaves and close growth, with a pungent, slightly acid taste. 'Thai' basil is very perfumed with large wavy-edged leaves.

parsley Parsley (see bottom right) is a fabulously decorative plant, and its intense colour and clear, fresh flavour can be available all year from an early spring sowing.

tarragon Arguably the most distinctive and for many the most desirable summer herb is tarragon. French tarragon, a perennial plant with lax growth and long, skinny leaves is the one to go for. Plants cannot be raised from seed so this is one of the 'pass it on herbs', propagated by division. It is slightly tender and worth protecting with a cloche or digging up, potting and bringing into a cold greenhouse or the porch for the winter.

The leaves can be stripped from the stem or they can be taken individually. You can add sprigs to wine vinegar for a wonderful tarragon-infused vinegar that lasts for months.

fennel and dill Two members of the carrot family, fennel and dill, are favourite summer herbs. Both have a pronounced aniseed flavour and combine wonderfully with fish. They also make important constituents of sauces and herb butters but need to be chopped finely. The seeds of both are used as digestifs, in pickles and as flavouring.

basil pesto

By summer, parsley is well away, followed by marjoram (also called oregano) and tarragon. Basil won't start until it is really warm, but in a short space of time it is so prolific that you can have lots to go at. Pesto is one way of storing it, but you can also use it fresh with extravagance.

makes 1 small pot
2 garlic cloves
sea salt and black pepper (or 2 green peppercorns)
25g (1oz) pine nuts
1 tablespoon freshly grated Parmesan
125ml (4fl oz) extra virgin olive oil
1 large bowlful basil leaves

Peel and smash the garlic and grind in a pestle and mortar if you have one with a good pinch of salt and ground pepper (or the green peppercorns if you have them). Add the pine nuts and grated Parmesan and continue grinding. Add a little oil if you need it to keep things moving.

Chop the basil leaves with a rocking hachoir or sharp knife and put as much as you can in the pestle to grind in with the mixture. Fold the mixture into a bowl with the rest of the basil and add as much oil as gives you the texture you want.

If you can resist eating it all straight away, put it in a jar, flatten the top of the pesto and cover with a layer of olive oil. (The oil excludes the air and slows down the attack of air-borne fungus, which makes it go off, even in a fridge.)

sauce vert

This is a versatile mixture. For a hot sauce, add it to a hollandaise or sauce maltaise (see page 220). For a tepid sauce, add the sauce vert to a mayonnaise or a sauce rémoulade (see page 220). If using cold, add the green sauce to an ice-cream (see page 161).

makes enough for 4
450g (1lb) spinach
4 sprigs fresh tarragon
4 sprigs fresh parsley
1 good handful watercress and 1 good handful sorrel leaves if available, otherwise make up with light green-leaved herbs like chervil or dill

Strip away all the spinach and herb stalks and blanch the leaves in a pan of fast-boiling water for 2–3 minutes. Drain and squeeze out any remaining water.

Mash in a mortar and pestle or liquidize and strain through a mill or sieve.

sauce vert

autumn

tender vegetables

aubergine

From the Mediterranean to India, the aubergine (or 'brinjal', the king of vegetables) was the vehicle of choice for indulging despotic rulers with ostentatiously rich and elaborate recipes, such as the famous 'imam bayildi'.

growing aubergines

Aubergines are soft-skinned tropical fruits that just about grow in the UK. They will fruit under glass and even outside in sheltered sun-traps. The more exotic and tropical the aubergine, the more it depends on heat and high light levels to crop. Whether or not they will be successful is down to the kind of summer and micro-climate they get. For harvesting, see page 141.

preparing aubergines

To purge them of excess water and bitterness it is usually recommended that you cut them up, heavily salt them and leave them for an hour to drain off. If you don't bother to salt them in this way, it doesn't seem to make much difference to how much oil they will absorb (see below). If you grow your own, you can pick them young so they are not spongy or seedy inside, and they don't need salting.

culinary characteristics of aubergines

They have a bland flavour and are very absorbent, so barbecue smoke, garlic, herbs – strong flavours basically – will permeate them deeply. Unfortunately, they will also absorb prodigious amounts of oil when cooking. You start with enough oil to deep-fry them in slices and find yourself sautéing them. The oil has got to go somewhere, so it leaks out when the aubergines are on the plate.

roasting or baking aubergines

A better alternative to frying aubergines is to roast or bake them instead. Cooked like this, they don't need much oil and remain sweet and fresh when they are soft and tender. Even for ratatouille it is a good idea to pre-roast them before combining them with the other vegetables, because they will still absorb all the other flavours without becoming an oily mush, unless of course you want a soft, stewed-down ratatouille. To roast aubergines, cut them in half if they are about the size of an apple, or into long segments, like an orange, if they are any bigger. Oil a baking tray and brush the exposed surfaces of the aubergines with oil. In a moderately hot oven (about 190°C/375°F/Gas 5), bake them for about 20–40 minutes. It might be necessary to cover them with a plate or some foil for the first half of the baking to stop them drying out or burning on the corners.

'With a good British summer – sunny, bright and warm – all these crops can do well outside without glass cover.'

picking aubergines, chillies and peppers

We think of aubergines, chillies and peppers as exotic plants that can only be grown under glass. This gives them a longer harvesting season, with chillies and peppers still harvestable past the early frosts and even into December. However, with a good sunny, bright and warm British summer, all these crops can do well outside without glass cover, especially if situated in a sunny, sheltered spot.

All these plants (and tomatoes too) stop flowering, and therefore making new fruit, when they reach their full 'fruit load'. You can delay this point by harvesting single fruits as and when they ripen. If you remove red fruits before they become fully ripe, the plant will try to have another go and make new ones.

when and how to harvest aubergines
Aubergines are best picked young, as overly mature ones become woolly, with a large pithy centre full of bitter brown seeds. Fruits should be cut off with an inch of stalk, using a sharp knife or secateurs. Fruits should be glossy. Some gardeners recommend waiting until your

Aubergines, chillies and peppers stop flowering and therefore making fruit, when they reach their full 'fruit load'.

thumbnail leaves an indentation when pressed into the side before cutting, but it is better too early than too late. An over-ripe aubergine will have a dull skin and will feel soft.

when and how to harvest chillies
Chillies change colour as they ripen, so it helps to know what colour they are meant to be. Most chillies are red when they are ripe and go red straight from green or via yellow and orange. Size and ripeness do not always go together and many fruits reach full size before they ripen; some chillies, even when all are fully ripe, will be an assortment of sizes. Fruits should be cut off with a sharp knife or secateurs, taking care not to snap the brittle stalks. Most chillies are so hot that you don't have to wait for full ripeness, and any extra sweetening will not be noticed. The most

Most chillies get to their full size before they start changing colour and ripening, however an unripe green chilli of a very hot variety (above right) will be more fiery than a ripe and red chilli of a milder variety (above left).

concentrated capsaicinoids are in the membrane around the seeds, but squirts of oil can come out of the fruit from rough handling. They are not water-soluble, so milk, yoghurt or alcohol should be used first in an emergency.

when and how to harvest sweet peppers

Sweet peppers go through the traffic light colours in reverse to reach full ripeness. A green pepper will be unripe, but it will certainly be crisp and succulent. Most people harvest peppers according to their size, valuing the crispness. By the time a pepper is deep red, the skin will be softer and the flesh will be less crisp.

The longer a sweet pepper is on the plant, the sweeter it becomes. This red fruit will be softer and sweeter than its green counterparts.

moutabal

Large aubergines are best overcooked and soft. They are especially good barbecued on a rack or best on wood embers. The skin can char completely but still hold together enough to ensure the middle is soft. A little nick of the skin lets it stretch during cooking. This recipe comes from the Middle East.

serves 2–4 as a dip
3 small aubergines
extra virgin olive oil
1 garlic clove
sea salt and black pepper
2 dessertspoons tahini (a sesame paste, available in jars)
juice of 1 lemon

Barbecue or grill the aubergines until the middles are soft, about 20 minutes.

Put a little oil in a big mixing bowl and get ready something to wipe your fingers. Wipe the carbon or dust off the aubergines (some people run them under a cold tap). Put one at a time in the bowl and scrape out the soft insides. Discard the skins but at least you have now maximized the barbecue flavour into the bowl. A messy job but finger-licking good.

Peel and mash the garlic with a little salt in a mortar. Add 3 tablespoons of the oil, the tahini and lemon juice, alternating each to make it easy. Fork into the aubergine pulp. Eat with pitta bread.

aubergine stuffed with rice & mint

Aubergines have a full but mild taste that can carry a wide range of other flavours with it, so there is more than just rice in this stuffing.

serves 3
3 fat aubergines
fine sea salt
1 onion, peeled
¼ fennel bulb (optional)
2 garlic cloves, peeled
150g (5½oz) butter or 3 tablespoons olive oil
1 small courgette
a good 100g (3½oz) arborio or carnaroli rice
10 fresh mint leaves
1 bunch fresh coriander, leaves chopped
3 fresh chive stalks and flowers, chopped

Preheat the oven to 190°C/375°F/Gas 5.

Cut the aubergines lengthways in half. Spoon out the centres, reserving the flesh. Rub them with salt and turn them upside down to drain.

Chop the onion, fennel, if using, and garlic finely and stew in the butter or oil until soft. Grate the courgette and the aubergine core (if not too fibrous) and seeds and add to the pan. Add the rice and stir with the butter or oil.

Soak the mint leaves in 150ml (5fl oz) hot water for a couple of minutes and add to the pan. Add another 300ml (10fl oz) hot water. Cover and let the rice steam until cooked, adding more water and stirring as necessary.

Rinse out the aubergines and dry the cavity. Fill with the risotto (having stirred in the herbs), place on a baking tray and cover with foil.

Bake for 30–40 minutes, and sprinkle on more herbs before serving.

aubergine stuffed with rice & mint

chilli peppers

Chilli peppers are usually varieties of pepper from the group *Capsicum annuum,* which also includes sweet or bell peppers, the traffic-light peppers beloved of supermarkets. The milder hot chillies, such as 'jalapeño', tend to be *C. annuum*, while the hottest chillies tend to belong to close relatives: *C. frutescens* and *C. chinense*.

There has been an explosion of interest in chilli peppers recently and now there is a bewildering array of cultivars available. 'A bit of chilli' has become the default flavour of 'blokes doing the cooking'. Unfortunately this has resulted in an indiscriminate quest for naked heat, the cooking equivalent of having 'the hottest curry on the menu'. Interestingly, the heat of chillies was unknown in Indian cuisine before the importation of chilli peppers from the New World in the 17th century.

growing chillies

Chilli pepper bushes tend to be more compact than those of sweet peppers, having a lighter load of fruits to bear, and so they are more likely to get a good spot in a greenhouse or porch. They will grow and fruit outdoors in the UK, requiring a long season and as much shelter and sun as they can get, but they will relish the heat they can get under glass or plastic, especially if they are kept well watered. They will grow between 10–35°C (50–95°F) but thrive at 27°C (80°F) with high light levels. Planting into 3 litre pots will prevent them growing overly lush and vigorous.

For a novice grower, the variety 'Hungarian Hot Wax' is very reliable, giving a continuous supply of fruit late into autumn and beyond. The fruit start small and yellow-green and at this stage they are piquant and spicy but not particularly hot. The next stage is almost full size and orange and the heat is definitely there. Ripe and red and left to mature, the final stage qualifies it as a hot chilli. Thus you can tell when the chilli has reached your preferred heat by how ripe it is, and remove the chilli from the plant at that point. For harvesting, see page 140.

preparing and cooking chillies

It is very difficult to get the skin off a tiny chilli pepper. The hottest capsaicins are held in the ridge that holds the seeds; scraping this away with the seeds will reduce the heat. In a cooked dish, it is very difficult to get rid of excessive fieriness from chillies, even by adding yoghurt or coconut milk. It is better to add chillies bit by bit if possible so you don't reach the point of no return...

harissa paste

This is a hot, Moroccan inspired paste, that you will end up using to enliven all sorts of dishes (see runner beans with harissa paste, page 62).

makes plenty
300g (10½oz) mixed fresh chillies
1 dessertspoon caraway seeds
1 dessertspoon cumin seeds
½ teaspoon black cumin seeds (optional)
2 large garlic cloves, peeled
1 sun-dried tomato
1 tablespoon sherry vinegar
5 fresh mint leaves
¼ teaspoon smoked paprika
200ml (7 fl oz) olive oil

Prepare the chillies as for pickled chillies (see right). Toast the spice seeds together in a dry pan on a medium-high heat for 40 seconds, then crush them in a pestle and mortar.

Put all the ingredients, including the chillies and toasted spices, in a blender. Blend to mix, then transfer to a pan and gently simmer for 10 minutes. (At this point, you can add another 300ml/10fl oz olive oil. This you can drain off later, when it will be full of the harissa flavours as well as a chilli kick, and can be used separately.)

Put the harissa paste in a clean glass jar and keep the surface covered with a layer of oil. Shake the jar after each use, keep in the fridge and use within three weeks.

quick pickled chillies with olive oil & garlic

Home-grown chillies can have a piquant flavour so long as it is not blown all away by the intense heat of the capsaicins. Instead of growing extreme varieties for their kick, grow milder ones and use more of them.

serves 2–4
1 garlic clove
1 tablespoon honey
sherry vinegar to cover, about 75ml (2½fl oz)
4 red chillies
4 green chillies

Smash the garlic and remove the skin. Put it in a small pan with the honey and half the vinegar.

Cut the tops off the chillies. Slit the chillies in half lengthways. Keeping your fingers clear, scrape the pale pith and the seeds out with a small sharp knife or, better still, a pointy teaspoon. Scrape away from you to avoid wet pith shooting up into your eyes. Save the seeds for next year's crop. Cut the chilli strips in half if they look too big for one mouthful.

Bring the pan containing the honey and vinegar to a rolling boil, stirring. Put in the chillies and just cover with the rest of the vinegar. Reduce the heat and simmer. By the time the vinegar has just about evaporated and the liquor is shiny and sticky but still liquid, the peppers will be done – munchy, not crunchy.

quick pickled chillies with olive oil & garlic

VARIETIES

Choose peppers that mature early; the earliest will bear fewer and smaller fruits, the later ones will bear more and bigger ones.

GRILLING AND ANTIPASTO PEPPERS 'DOLCE DI BERGAMO', 'FRIGATELLO'.

STUFFING PEPPERS 'CORNO ROSSO', 'TOPEPO'.

SWEETEST PEPPERS 'GIALLO D'ASTI', 'LOMBARDIA', 'DULCE ITALIANO'.

sweet peppers

There is an enormous range of peppers, botanically *Capsicum annuum*, whether fleshy and sweet (which we call 'sweet' or 'bell' peppers) or small and fiery ('chilli' peppers).

the colours of sweet peppers

Most green peppers are 'unripe', and as they mature, they go from green to yellow to orange then red, or from green to green mixed with red, then to red. At the dark red stage, the seeds are ripe and ready. If the pepper is a hot variety, the riper the seed the hotter it is. Green peppers are attractive and crunchy, but tend to be more bitter and less sweet than fully ripe ones. A green pepper with a thin wall of skin and flesh is more useful and digestible than a variety with a thick wall, but less crunchy and succulent.

Some specialized peppers have been bred to be yellow, orange, purple or chocolate brown in their early stages. Shapes go from blunt and chunky to mean and pointy, generally getting hotter as they shrink in size; this is bred into them from the outset.

growing sweet peppers

In the UK, peppers sometimes struggle to get enough heat and light outside and do better under glass or plastic, cropping about a month earlier in June or July. Choose peppers that set fruits early as these have a better chance of ripening over the summer. Pepper fruit can hang off the bush well into November if under cover, though the wall will have shrunk quite a bit and the bush looks totally exhausted. For harvesting, see page 141.

eating raw sweet peppers

With sweet peppers, you are not waiting for the heat inside to develop as with chillies; ripeness comes when the pepper develops sufficient sweetness and has attained the size and colour you want. Ideally a sweet pepper has a thin skin and thick succulent flesh. The skin will hold the raw pepper together if the flesh is young, crisp and thin when you slice it, but the knife must be sharp. Many people find raw peppers quite indigestible, but then others like their colour and crunchiness in salads.

skinning/cooking sweet peppers

Mature peppers will have stronger skins and thicker flesh. These are better cooked than raw and sometimes it is best to get the skin off first. You have to burn the skin to char it before you can rub it off, and you can do this with charcoal, gas hobs, blow-torches and even candles. Try to blacken the skin evenly all over without softening the flesh underneath. Then place the hot peppers on a plate in a plastic bag, or in a pan or plastic box with a tight lid. The steam that comes off will help loosen the skins. Alternatively hold them under running cold water or rub them with a tea-towel to get the carbon off.

The soft flesh of well-cooked roast peppers will fall away from the skin if you gently scrape it, though you don't always collect all the skin, or keep the pepper flesh intact.

roast peppers with olive oil, garlic & oregano

Why don't we burn the skin off the peppers? On a standard industrial greenhouse pepper that's been touring the country in a box for a fortnight, who would want to eat the skin? But on a home-grown pepper, still throbbing with life just ten minutes ago, the skin is delectable and as integral a part of what it is to eat a pepper as the yielding flesh.

serves 4–6

4 large or 6 medium peppers
3 garlic cloves
75ml (2½fl oz) olive oil
6 sprigs fresh oregano
sea salt and black pepper

Preheat the oven to 190°C/375°F/Gas 5.

Cut the top and bottom off each pepper. Put a sharp knife against the inside of one pepper ring and follow the circle all the way round; this will sever the pith holding the seeds from the ring of flesh. Save the seeds for next year's crop. Repeat with all the peppers.

Cut each ring of pepper into three or four sections. Also detach the stalks from the flesh of the top of the peppers so you can use the top and bottom of the peppers as well.

Smash the garlic cloves and remove the skins. Pour some of the oil onto a baking tray and cover both sides of the peppers with oil. Sprinkle the garlic, oregano, salt and pepper over them, bunch them up in the tray and pour on the remaining oil.

Roast, basting occasionally, for 15–20 minutes. Home-grown cook a lot quicker.

peppers with couscous

Red and green peppers look good with the pale yellow couscous. They can be presented as pieces within the couscous or they can be stuffed with it.

serves 4

1 green and 1 red pepper
1 onion or 3 spring onions
1 mild chilli pepper (optional)
1¼ tablespoons extra virgin olive oil
1 tablespoon rinsed and drained capers
1 bunch fresh parsley, finely chopped
1 teaspoon pomegranate syrup
2 teaspoons balsamic vinegar
sea salt and black pepper
115g (4oz) couscous, cooked (follow instructions on the packet)

Deseed and destalk the peppers, and cut the flesh into 1cm (½in) strips. Chop the onion or spring onions into a similar size and mince the chilli, if using.

Soften the onions gently in the oil, then add both types of peppers, the chilli, capers and parsley. Dissolve the syrup and vinegar in 150ml (5fl oz) very hot water and add to the pan. Check the seasoning, then simmer for a few minutes until the peppers are munchy.

Empty the cooked couscous into the pan, stir it all around and empty into a serving dish.

peppers with couscous

VARIETIES

PUMPKIN **'ROUGE VIF D'ETAMPS'** is a nice reddish one.

BUTTERNUT SQUASH **'WALTHAM'** and **'COBNUT'** have moist, nutty flesh.

BUTTERCUP SQUASH **'BURGESS VINE BUTTERCUP'** is sweet but full-flavoured.

ACORN SQUASH **'THELMA SANDERS SWEET POTATO'** is very early and lasts well too.

BANANA SQUASH The grey-green **'BLUE BANANA'** grows up to 60cm (2ft) long.

HUBBARD SQUASH **'ANNA SWARTZ HUBBARD SQUASH'** is a reliable green-skinned variety, with tasty, dense orange flesh.

---

winter squash
pumpkins & squashes

A winter squash can be almost any size, shape, pattern and colour, but it is always the star of any late harvest festival. It can also be called a pumpkin, and it can be an old summer squash with thickened skin and ripened flesh.

pumpkin

Pumpkins are those familiar orange giants with semi-hard skin, perfect for carving at Hallowe'en. The flesh is usually orange too, and the sweetest of the lot. In fact, it can be too sweet to be a savoury vegetable and the purée ends up in American pumpkin pie. Roasted with thyme and garlic until it collapses, it can make a one-off seasonal soup.

butternut squash

This has nice firm flesh that has to be cooked to tenderness all the way through. It needs a very long season to mature, so has to be started early. The cooked texture is satisfyingly tender and is excellent roasted, cut open in halves or quarters with olive oil, salt, rosemary and soft goat's cheese on top. The skin is thin and easy to peel.

buttercup squash

These are different again, with a sweet and creamy texture from less watery flesh. Skins tend to be tough and dark green, the fruits substantial but not monumental.

acorn squash

Acorn squashes are small and heart-shaped (almost like sweet peppers) with a hard, fluted rind, and are ideal cut in half and baked for two people. The seeds can be roasted.

banana squash

This is a fat cigar shape, tasty and golden-fleshed but above all vigorous and huge. The waxy skin is thin and peelable but it keeps well.

hubbard squash

The hard skin of these very large squashes is crinkled and warty. Early varieties can get in a good growing season whatever the weather, and are vigorous and productive.

cooking squashes

Overly sweet squashes in purées and soups can have their sweetness balanced by sharper-tasting celeriac, or thinned out by blander-tasting potatoes. Bay leaves, thyme, sage and garlic can also mitigate sweetness.

'Ripening on the vine is ideal, and the fruits should be fully supported from an early stage, even on a tile to keep them off wet soil.'

picking winter squash

The miracle of life is very evident in winter squashes. From one small seed an enormous runaway plant spreads out wide, depositing mammoth fruits. Happily, not all varieties are like that: most of them have relatively compact bushes, and some can trail up vertically with modest fruit that can be supported, hanging down, by the plant itself.

when to harvest winter squashes

Ripening is essential for the squash to last into winter after growing all through the summer. In Britain, 'early' varieties set flowers and fruit quickly so that the growing season is as long as possible. Ripening on the vine is the ideal, and the fruits should be fully supported from an early stage, even on a tile to keep them off wet soil. Leaves around squashes should be cut back in early autumn so that the fruits can bathe in all the sunshine going. If there is to be an occasional light frost, the squashes can be insulated at night with straw or hessian. Harvest the squashes when the cold sets in.

Members of the curcurbit family either turn to mush in weeks or toughen up and see out the winter.

how to cut winter squashes

The stalk should be cut either side of the vine, as a T-shape, and it should not be used as a carrying handle taking the weight of the squash: rot usually starts from damaged stalks.

how to store winter squashes

To be able to store the squashes into winter, the skin needs to finish toughening up and 'curing' to protect the flesh and stop it drying out. This takes about 10 days and usually has to happen indoors. Warmth helps curing and some growers keep their squashes at 25°C/77°F. Vigilance is required because excessive heat will cause them to shrivel. Once cured, the squashes can be kept in the cool, under 15°C/60°F (a shed or garage) until required. It is very important to let air circulate around the squashes, so huge piles should be avoided if there is room to spread them out, otherwise you will have to rotate them.

Squashes can be stored for use later in the year. A serrated knife cuts through hard skins (above).

To store squash, it needs to be ripe and nothing beats a long sunbathe (right). Keep it off damp soil.

Acorn squashes can be harvested meal by meal as they are the right size for a starter or an accompaniment (below).

squash & lentil tagine

If your squash cooks more quickly than the lentils, simply remove the squash when it is ready and return it to the pan to heat through near the end of the cooking time. This dish tastes great with couscous and yoghurt.

serves 4

250g (9oz) green lentils, soaked in water
1 medium onion, peeled
1 large garlic clove, peeled
1 slug olive oil
½ small pumpkin or 1 small squash
300ml (10fl oz) hot water
2 large teaspoons harissa paste (see page 146)
3 or 4 fresh mint, parsley or coriander
   leaves, chopped

If you can, soak the lentils in a bowl beforehand, for several hours at least.

Slice up the onion and gently fry with the smashed garlic in the olive oil.

Prepare the pumpkin or squash as for roast pumpkin gratin (see right), and cut the flesh into fork-sized chunks without skin. Turn these pieces in the oily onions. After a few minutes, tip in the drained lentils and stir. When the lentils are well hot, pour in the hot water and stir in the harissa paste.

Transfer to an ovenproof dish with a tight-fitting lid, ideally a clay tagine, and continue the cooking in a low oven. Check often, adding more hot water to stop the lentils drying out, until they and the vegetables are soft, about 35 minutes. Leave to stand for a few minutes with the chopped mint, parsley or coriander stirred in.

roast pumpkin gratin

You can roast squashes, marrows or pumpkins under this oily gratin.

serves 4

3 garlic cloves, peeled
coarse sea salt
extra virgin olive oil
55g (2oz) Parmesan, freshly grated
55g (2oz) ciabatta or stale white breadcrumbs
leaves from 1 sprig fresh thyme
1 pumpkin, marrow or squash about 1.8kg
   (4lb) in weight

Preheat the oven to 180°C/350°F/Gas 4.

Mash the peeled garlic with a good pinch of salt, preferably in a mortar. Add a stream of olive oil – about 25ml (1fl oz) – and work up an emulsion. If necessary transfer to a bigger bowl. Mix in the Parmesan, then the breadcrumbs and the loose leaves of the thyme.

Cut open the pumpkin and scrape out all the seeds and the fibrous flesh with a dessertspoon. If using a marrow or a squash with a thin skin, cut into large chunks; if the skin is thick or when using a pumpkin, peel off the skin before cutting into chunks.

Arrange the pieces in a baking tray flesh-side up and smear the oily mixture all over the top. Drizzle with a little extra oil and bake, covered with foil or a lid, in the preheated oven to get the heat right into the centre of the pieces.

After 20 minutes or so, when the flesh has just begun to feel very nearly soft to a poke with a sharp knife, take off the cover. Put the oven up to 200°C/400°F/Gas 6 and finish off for 10 minutes.

roast pumpkin gratin

bulbs

fennel

Florence fennel combines good looks, marvellous texture and delectable taste in one package. It is a fast-growing Mediterranean member of the Umbel family, with a fat, pale, edible bulb, long stems, feathery foliage and small, starry yellow flowers.

growing fennel

The ideal fennel has been grown very quickly: the bulb is fat and plump, the layers are crisp and juicy, and the leaves are tender. Mediterranean conditions are perfect for quick, uninterrupted growth. Further north, as in Britain, the plant grows more slowly, so the layers tend to be thinner, drier and tougher and the leaves quite tough in comparison.

Even, or maybe especially, in Britain, uninterrupted growth is most important. Fennel plants are quite sensitive and, if they suffer unexpected reversals like cold snaps or water-stress, they tend to 'bolt', that is put all their energy into growing a main stem and as many seeds as they can manage.

Seeds for fennel should be sown when the likelihood of very cold nights has gone, late May in most places. Fennel hates root disturbance, so a good way to avoid transplanting is to plant two seeds in a module, taking out the weakest if they both germinate, and set out the young plant when it is fairly sturdy.

harvesting fennel

The bulb can be dug up for harvesting by loosening the roots with a small fork and pulling the whole plant out of the ground. Or the bulb can be cut horizontally across just above the soil level to encourage new feathery sprouts useful as a garnish.

preparing fennel

The roots can be cut off just above the soil-level ring, which takes off the coarse base as well. For salads and other raw uses, it is the Italian practice to slice the bulb very thinly, horizontally across, so the interlocking layers are all very short and cross-cut, not long and fibrous. This makes chewing and digestion easier. For roasting or braising, the bulb can be cut into quarters vertically between the stems.

eating and cooking fennel

The bulb is hard and crunchy, it is surprisingly moreish eaten raw, especially, but it can be excellent roasted or braised slowly. The stems are a disappointment though. They are just about of use for flavouring soups, sauces or stews and they can have an improvised use as barbecue skewers. However 'Romanesco' and 'Fennel di Parma sel. Prado' have crunchy 'full canes' or stems. The foliage is wispy yet quite tough, but full of aniseed flavour. The thin tips can be used raw, wilted or lightly sautéed for a garnish. The flowers can be stripped off their stalks and used as a garnish.

fennel & potato stew with herb ice-cream

Home-grown fennel has a very fresh taste, enhanced by a summery 'stew' of lightly cooked vegetables from the garden.

serves 2

350g (12oz) waxy new potatoes
1 large fennel bulb
1 medium carrot
1 sprig fresh tarragon (optional)
3 fresh mint leaves
1 sprig fresh parsley
1 small bunch fresh chives
2 large handfuls podded peas or broad beans, or both

Herb ice-cream

4 medium egg yolks
425ml (15fl oz) milk or single cream
1 recipe *sauce vert* (see page 132)

For the herb ice-cream, beat the egg yolks in a bowl. Bring the milk or cream to the boil and pour into the yolks, stirring all the time. Return it to the pan over a moderate heat, stirring until it thickens. Allow to cool, but stir frequently to prevent a skin forming.

Freeze the cold custard and, if you check it, give it another stir. When it is set, but not a block of ice, stir in the *sauce vert* mixture, then return it to the freezer. Put in the fridge just before serving so you can cut it easily.

Scrub the potatoes, cut them in half and put them in the steamer first. Quarter the fennel bulb and chop the carrot into chunks. After 5 minutes, add the fennel and herbs. After another 5 minutes, add the carrots, peas and/or beans.

After about 5 minutes, serve with a scoop of the herb ice-cream.

fennel & potato stew with herb ice-cream

caramelized fennel

Fennel is incredibly useful, not only for its bright, fresh aniseedy flavour, but also its crunchiness. It lends itself very well to slicing across the bulb, so the slices can be very fine and easily digestible, however coarse and thick the rings (they make a good addition to a pizza topping). For a softer, sweeter incarnation, try this caramelized recipe.

serves 2

2 fat fennel bulbs
50ml (2fl oz) olive oil
sea salt and black pepper

Cut the fennel bulbs into 1cm (½in) horizontal rings. If you think they will be too big, cut the bulb in half vertically first, so you have semi-circles.

Heat the oil in a large heavy pan, to moderately hot. Before the oil smokes, put in the fennel. Sauté for nearly 10 minutes, agitating the pan to make sure the fennel doesn't scorch and turning it over in the oil. Drain well and season.

roots

celeriac

You're don't often come across celeriac in the shops, so what is it? *Apium graveolens* var. *rapaceum*, an ugly rooty bulb about the size of a big grapefruit. The leafy stems shooting vertically upright are celery stalks; instead of the familiar tight bunch, there are fewer of them and they are more spread out in the varieties selected as celeriac.

growing celeriac

As they grow, peel off the outer stems to encourage the root to swell. You must make sure that the celeriac gets plenty of water because it likes it as damp as possible and the ideal bulb is dense and heavy.

Late in the growing season, and to see them through into winter if you're storing them in the ground, you should open them out even more by taking off nearly all the stems. This gives marauding slugs fewer places to lurk. However, if there is a likelihood of freezing, you may choose to lift them and store them in an earth or sand clamp or mulch them, say with straw. If the risk is only for the occasional frost, you can leave the bulbs in the soil, letting the stems flop and taking them off to prevent rot until you need the root.

harvesting celeriac

The bulbs are ready to be lifted when they have reached the size of an orange but before they are the size of a Galia melon. They don't really have a tender young stage when they must be eaten small, but they do have a stage when they get so big they get internal cavities and a woolly coarseness. They also get bitter and fibrous if they have undergone high heat, drought or water-stress. They like it cool and continuously damp.

preparing celeriac

After chopping off the top and bottom of the bulb with roots and shoots attached, celeriac needs peeling of the muddy, fissured skin, knobbled with dud stems. Once the inner flesh is exposed to air, it can turn from cream to grey in colour. To prevent this it should be used quickly or stored in acidulated water (that is, with a big squeeze of lemon juice).

cooking and eating celeriac

The stems of celeriac are too coarse usually to eat as a crudité, as you would with celery stalks. They can, however, be used with leaves still on for flavouring cooked dishes and soups (and removed before eating).

Raw celeriac is crisp, succulent and fully but mildly flavoured of celery and slightly of fennel/aniseed. Traditionally, raw celeriac is served in little julienne strips about the size of thick matchsticks – the French mix them into a grain mustardy mayonnaise for rémoulade (see page 220) – or in flat chunks the size of one-pound coins.

Lightly cooked celeriac has a firm but tender texture that marries well with potatoes and other root vegetables, as in a roast or a hearty gratin. Well-cooked celeriac mashes well, combining nicely with other mashed roots, though it is lighter and more watery than, say, potatoes.

celeriac & beetroot salad

Cooking celeriac for the first time can be a revelation. It cooks kindly, and because it can grow or be stored through the winter, it can become very useful. It can be poached à la grecque (see page 36), and shares many recipes with cauliflowers and artichokes.

serves 4

1 small young celeriac bulb
4 or 5 young beetroots
1 fennel bulb, if available
1 shallot, peeled and halved
1 sprig fresh tarragon
1 bunch fresh dill
1 tablespoon extra virgin olive oil
juice of 1 small lemon
sea salt and black pepper

Peel the celeriac bulb down to clean flesh and cut into chunks the same size as your young beetroot. Then slice them very thinly, about 3mm (⅛in) thick. Slice across the fennel bulb in the same way. Slice the peeled and halved shallot the same way too. Toss together the white vegetables like shuffling cards.

Chop the herb leaves finely and in a serving bowl mix them with the oil, most of the lemon juice and a pinch of salt. Toss the white vegetables with the dressing.

Top, tail and peel the beetroot (use the stems and leaves shredded for a salad or wilted as an accompaniment), then slice them equally thin. You do them last because you don't want everything to end up pink like a load of whites washed with a pair of red knickers.

Shuffle the beetroot slices, then fold them through the rest of the salad and grind on some black pepper.

roast tandoori celeriac

This can be roasted or even barbecued, so it is just beginning to char outside but yield inside.

serves 4

1 large or 3–4 baby celeriac bulbs
3 large dessertspoons bought tandoori paste, or home-made (see below)
about 200g (7oz) plain yoghurt
1 tablespoon melted butter or ghee
Tandoori paste
1 teaspoon each of cumin, mustard and black onion seeds
1 dessertspoon grated fresh root ginger
1 dessertspoon olive oil
2 tablespoons harissa paste (see page 146)

If you want to make the tandoori paste yourself, heat the spice seeds in a dry pan until they pop (but before they burn – it can happen quickly and they carry on cooking off the heat). Grind them in a mortar and pestle and add them with the ginger to the oil. Heat gently and, when the ginger is sizzling and turning colour, stir in the harissa paste and blend together.

Peel the celeriac and cut it into large knobbly chunks. Mix 3 large dessertspoons of the tandoori paste in a bowl with the plain yoghurt. Coat the celeriac in the mixture and leave overnight, covered in the fridge, to marinate.

Preheat the oven to 220°C/425°F/Gas 7.

Heat the butter or ghee in a pan and add the celeriac and marinade, having stirred the marinade to recoat the celeriac. Turn into a roasting dish, and roast the celeriac in the hot oven or barbecue for 15–30 minutes.

roast tandoori celeriac

turnips

The turnip of traditional British cooking and agricultural history is a dull old thing. At best, it can be boiled soft and mashed with – stereotypical Scottish recipe – butter, sugar and salt and called 'neeps'. At worst, it can be a smelly muddy pile of inedible lumps in a farmer's shed. Turnips are *Brassica napus*, and the memory of the sweet-smelling flowers is quite negated by the terror of the old rotting roots.

growing turnips

If ever there was a difference between a commercial crop and a grow-your-own vegetable, turnips are a great illustration. Baby young turnips are fresh and crisp with barely a skin, and they cook in a trice. Shop-bought turnips lose their crispness quickly and go from undercooked to overcooked and bitter very quickly.

Some varieties of turnip crop almost as quickly as radishes and two crops a year – one in spring and a quick one in autumn – can be better than one dragged out for a whole season, spring to autumn. This way, small sowings can fill the odd gap in planting, either (in space) between rows or (in time) between crops.

Turnips benefit from steady growing in cool conditions in spring or autumn; drought and heat make them bitter, thick-skinned and woolly, with a woody centre if they bolt.

cooking young turnips

The leaves of most turnips can be eaten as steamed greens, but it is essential to catch them young and tender before a coarse flavour overtakes them. Young turnips can be steamed, sautéed and stir-fried when small, still with their green tops on, or sliced. An oily roast with other root vegetables such as parsnips, carrots, celeriac and beetroot is so good it deserves to have small tender new turnips to join them rather than lumps of salvaged old survivors. Turnips in stews used to conjure up images of massive submerged dumplings, but now a little golf-ball bobbing around in a light springtime ragoût is more attractive an image.

cooking more mature turnips

There is so much else to eat in the middle of the year that the humble turnip often gets overlooked. Golf balls become egg-sized. The larger the turnip the less likely it is to go spongy, but then the less appetizing it is, so the less point there is to store it. Medium-sized turnips can be roasted after peeling, especially varieties with 'nutty' flavours: test for doneness with a fork rather than a sharp knife. Intense and robust flavours that make the turnip taste mild in combination seem to work best.

A main-crop turnip grown through summer will get bigger than a tennis ball. Not just the skin, but a little way in, will have to be taken off before cooking. Just how thick the peelings need to be depends on how coarse and fibrous the turnip is.

turnips in garlic sauce

This old French recipe gives the workaday turnip a more sophisticated persona.

serves 4

2 handfuls baby turnips or a few old ones
3 tablespoons olive oil
3 garlic cloves
sea salt and black pepper
1 tablespoon balsamic vinegar
1 bunch parsley, chopped

Peel the turnips if they are coarse and cut into quarters. Steam or blanch them in a pan of boiling salted water for a few minutes.

Heat the oil in a heavy pan with a lid and tip in the turnips. Let them simmer gently with the lid on for about 8 miutes.

Smash and peel the garlic and grind to a paste with some salt. Add the vinegar to this mixture, and when the turnips are tender, tip the mixture into the turnip pan. Stir it all around to blend the liquor and sprinkle on the parsley to serve.

stir-fry turnips

Fresh baby turnips with paper-thin skins and crisp flesh are unknown to the shopper but an anticipated treat to the gardener. As such a delicacy, simply rolling them around a pan with some good butter, then some water and a tight lid is enough. When more mature you need to peel and slow cook as a root vegetable rather than as a crisp radish.

serves 2

6 baby turnips
3 spring onions
2 garlic cloves
1 small red chilli
1 x 5cm (2in) piece fresh root ginger
2 dessertspoons vegetable oil, groundnut ideally
soy sauce (tamari or light)

Top and tail the turnips and if not tiny, cut into fat flakes. Slice the onions diagonally, and peel and slice the garlic thinly. Deseed the chilli and slice into thin strips. Cut the skin off the ginger and slice thinly like the garlic.

Heat the oil in a wok and, when beginning to smoke, put in the onion. After a minute, add the garlic, chilli and ginger. Before the garlic changes colour, add the turnips. Splash in enough soy sauce to prevent burning and serve as soon as the turnips are crunchily edible, which is after about 4 minutes.

stir-fry turnips

leaves

chard

The coloured chards, with their stalks and ribs in vibrant yellow, orange and red, are worthy of inclusion in any planting scheme on the basis of their appearance alone, and have the added bonus of offering delicious eating. However, compared with the white or Swiss variety, they do not have the all-weather reliability and superb mild flavour.

harvesting chard

Chard plants have a long life. They can last a year or more and may be harvested right through their growing life. We take big individual leaves from a short row of plants; four or five are enough for two people. Some advocate cutting with a sharp knife, but the best method is to hold the plant firmly and pull the leaf gently at its base. In severe weather the outside leaves get a bit battered, but can be left to protect the inner ones.

preparing chard

The texture of the leaf is halfway between spinach and kale. It doesn't collapse like spinach when cooked, nor does it stay as tough as kale. It holds its shape, even when shredded, but is tender and yielding.

The texture of the stalk is just on the munchy side of crunchy. It is wholly different to the leaves and, even if you serve them together, it is better to cook them separately. The obvious thing is to rip all the leaf off the stalk, but if you only cut away the stalk where it is still hard and wide, the cooked leaf will have a more satisfying texture.

When washing the leaf with the stalk still attached under running water, be aware that the long ridges on the stalk act like very efficient gutters, channelling all the water on to your clothes.

eating chard raw

Chard can be eaten raw, treated as a cut-and-come-again leaf, so you sever individual leaves when plants are young (it has an intensely sweet taste at this stage, like beetroot, to which it is closely related), but it only develops its full flavour, earthy yet creamy, when it is mature. Baby coloured chard stalks and leaves can go raw into a salad to add colour and texture – and more successfully – quickly wilted as a side vegetable. White chard can do all that but it really comes into its own when it has grown on some more.

cooking chard

The cut-up stalk only requires 3 minutes' steaming, the coarsely shredded leaf only about 1 minute, so it is a simple matter to start steaming the stalk, then 2 minutes later add the leaf on top and steam for 1 more minute.

chard stem gratin

Chard is a good friend in the garden and in the kitchen. Standing out in all weathers, it still provides reliable supplies of tender leaves and substantial stems.

serves 4

3 or 4 large chard stems
2 garlic cloves
200ml (7fl oz) crème fraîche or double cream,
  or half and half
sea salt and black pepper
3 tablespoons ground almonds
1 teaspoon freshly grated Parmesan

Preheat the oven to 200°C/400°F/Gas 6.

Clean the chard and cut into 5cm (2in) lengths. If bits of green leaf are attached, this is a bonus. Peel the garlic and slice paper-thin.

Steam the chard interspersed with the garlic over fast-boiling salted water for 2 minutes.

If using both, mix together the cream and crème fraîche in the bottom of an ovenproof dish, warming it through in another pan first if you are in a hurry. Mix the chard into it, adding a little salt and plenty of pepper. Flatten the mixture in the bottom of the dish with a top layer of cream and cover with the ground almonds after working a pinch of salt through them. Sprinkle the Parmesan over the top.

Bake in the preheated oven for about 15 minutes, so it is all piping hot and the topping is nicely – but not too – browned. The nuts get browned off very quickly once they start colouring.

wilted chard with yoghurt & mascarpone

You can eat steamed chard leaves plain, with a vinaigrette dressing or a little butter, or with a yoghurt sauce as here.

serves 2–4

3 or 4 large chard leaves
115g (4oz) mascarpone cheese
115g (4oz) plain, preferably strained, Greek-
  style yoghurt
1 large pinch of freshly grated nutmeg

Wash the chard leaves, then pull the green leaves from the stalks. Cut the stalks across about 5mm (¼in) wide. If the stem is very wide, split it lengthways first. Steam them over boiling water for 2 minutes. Cut the leaves across about 1cm (½in) wide, add to the stems and steam for another minute.

For the yoghurt sauce, beat the mascarpone in a serving bowl, then fold in the yoghurt. Coat the chard all over with this, then sprinkle with the nutmeg.

wilted chard with yoghurt & mascarpone

winter

VARIETIES

'NOISETTE', 'EARLY HALF TALL' and 'SEVEN HILLS' are good varieties.

cabbage family
brussels sprouts

Brussels sprouts (*Brassica oleracea* var. *gemmifera*) are a winter-cropping brassica, familiar at Christmas time. They need very cold weather if not freezing to develop their full sweet, nutty flavour.

growing brussels sprouts

They will stand out in the garden through the summer into autumn, winter and even spring, as big as a sculpture. The soil around the stems of brussels sprouts should be kept firm in order to keep the plants well anchored. This can be achieved by regularly firming the ground with your foot. This firming-in also keeps the sprout buds firm, and helps prevent the sprouts from getting 'blown', loose-leafed and hollow. It is better to cut off the sprouts when they are tight, small, hard and heavy, than to wait until you can twist them off if they will be blown.

harvesting brussels sprouts

Take them off the stalk from the bottom up. This will give you a few at a time over maybe half a dozen pickings. If you want a Christmas blow-out, you can get them all ready at the same time by cutting off the top, leaves and all, in early autumn. (These leaves are a pleasant enough cabbage green.) If you want to crop the whole stalk, pull the whole plant out. This will reduce the risk of club root contaminating the soil.

preparing brussels sprouts

Standard practice is to pull off the loose leaves around the stem. When you have your own home-grown sprouts this is unnecessary, especially as the greenest leaves are these outer ones. Weather-worn leaves around the top of the bud are also often removed, but unless they look revolting, it will deprive you of the best bit. To make the inner core cook through at the same rate as the outer leaves, many cooks cut a cross in the base of the sprout. Since cooked sprouts don't have to be a uniform boiled mush, what's wrong with a difference in texture between the inside and outside of the sprout?

boiling/steaming brussels sprouts

Sprouts can be boiled whole but they are less likely to be overdone if they're steamed for around 5 minutes. They can be cut in half vertically and steamed for about 4 minutes if you are afraid the outer leaves will be mushy before the inner cores are cooked, but that is affected by what variety they are.

other cooking methods

You can use the leaves individually, apart from the ones around the very core. Cut out the core from the sprout and separate the leaves by pulling them apart in opposite directions. It will look a bit like a pile of flower petals and will cook very quickly.

Sprouts can be treated in the same way as cabbages – they are just miniaturized. They can be cut through finely to shred them (when they can be eaten raw in salads). They can even be stuffed if you've got tweezers.

'Take them off the stalk from the bottom up. This will give you a few at a time over maybe half a dozen pickings.'

Brussels sprouts mature on the stalk from the bottom upwards and should be harvested in this order.

pulling brassicas

Brussels sprouts have traditionally been harvested sprout by sprout because they were a winter stand-by, eaten continuously with diminishing relish. Nowadays, Christmas shoppers show off their stalks, completely covered in a spiral of sprouts.

Allotmenteers used to bear enormous cabbages home, to be eaten to the bitter end by all the family. Nowadays, we can find a meal or two from judicious picking of the outer leaves if we can't eat it all in one go, at the peak of its freshness.

when and how to harvest cabbages

Pick off cabbage leaves in good condition one at a time: three or four plants supply plenty for a meal. Fresh-picked cabbage is always best.

However, when you want a substantial heart on a cabbage, the time comes to cut the whole head off. In spring and summer, it is worth cutting a vertical cross about half an inch deep into the stump. Where the cabbage head once was, a cluster of new cabbage heads should form. If nothing shows after six weeks, pull out the whole stem. Roots of harvested brassicas rot away very slowly and invite soil-borne diseases, like clubroot. They should be removed and burnt rather than put on the compost heap.

when and how to harvest brussels sprouts

Brussels sprouts mature on the stalk from the bottom upwards and this is the usual order to pick them, As long as the sprouts are not open and 'blown', the upper ones can wait. However, sometimes it is nice to have very tight little sprouts to use whole as miniature cabbages. In this case it is not easy to pick them off with a sharp twist to the right or left. You will have to use a small sharp knife and cut them off the stalk with a controlled downwards motion. Supermarkets and shopkeepers think sprouts keep well but the gardeners who pick their own wouldn't recognize their sad offerings.

Many home gardeners are rediscovering the joy of brassicas when they have grown, harvested and tasted their own.

brussels sprout salad

Bubble and squeak on Boxing Day is a culinary highlight for us; for this, yesterday's Brussels sprouts are essential. Nowadays sprouts have emerged from their Christmas stigma, especially if they are viewed as baby cabbages instead. Here is the opposite of bubble and squeak – a salad of Brussels sprouts, raw.

serves 4
450g (1lb) young small Brussels sprouts
sweet and sour dressing
1 tablespoon each of unsweetened apple juice and pomegranate syrup
¼–½ teaspoon chopped red chilli flesh or harissa paste (see page 146)
balsamic vinegar, to adjust the balance

Clean up the sprouts and cut into 3mm (⅛in) slices. Halve tiny ones.

Mix all the ingredients for the dressing thoroughly in a bowl. Saturate the raw sprouts with the dressing. Add some chopped chilli to garnish and serve.

scrumping sprouts

This way of cooking sprouts keeps the bright green, peppery freshness of the sprouts but tempers their 'brassicaciousness' with a mellow sweetness.

serves 4
1kg (2¼lb) Brussels sprouts
1 small onion or shallot
1 eating apple, preferably Cox or similarly flavourful
55g (2oz) butter
125ml (4fl oz) cloudy apple juice
125ml (4fl oz) dry cider (as little industrialized as possible)

Take any damaged leaves off the sprouts but leave as many of the dark green leaves intact as you can.

Peel and dice the onion and apple and sweat gently in the butter until soft. Add apple juice as necessary to this while cooking to prevent frying or burning.

Tip in the sprouts and the rest of the apple juice on a high heat with the lid closed. Add the cider as necessary to keep the sprouts boiling in cider but not drowning. By the time they are cooked *al dente* – about 5 minutes – the liquor should be reduced to a lively sauce.

brussels sprout salad

cabbages

The cabbage family, *Brassica oleracea,* is huge and this has allowed breeders to create some very specific and individual cabbages. Most people are familiar with the two extremes: Dutch 'white' cabbage, very tight, dense balls of tasteless pale-green leaves or, in contrast, the open, floppy, puckered rosette of dark green Savoy cabbages.

There is a huge range in between with little commercial use, but of great value to the home-grower. It is possible to eat cabbages all year round, by harvesting different varieties successively throughout the year.

spring cabbages Spring cabbages are sown in late summer to early autumn, traditionally August and September, left to sulk over winter and then accelerate into spring and mature over the following six weeks. This is a comforting vegetable to eat cooked heartily while you are waiting for spring to warm up. Spring cabbages often have pointy, conical heads.

bok-choy or pak-choi Both of these Chinese cabbages (which are the same, *Brassica rapa,* except one comes in boxes, the other in packets) can be eaten raw even if they heart up or bolt, as can their young flowers. Tat-soi is a type with very dark leaves in flat rosettes, also known as 'Flat Black Cabbage'. These types have soft-celled leaves so sitting them in an oil and vinegar dressing for 10 minutes will quite wilt them.

summer cabbages Summer cabbages are sown in spring and have thin leaves that grow very quickly, full of vitality. They are good when used in robust salads, eaten raw, particularly in coleslaw, or steamed or sautéed very lightly.

winter cabbages These are sown in spring and early summer and, as autumn fades, they begin to bulk up and grow hearts that will survive the wintry weather. The crinkly, puckered Savoy cabbages have a surprising resistance to terrible weather, though they seem less sweet or spicy than drumheads. Savoy cabbage is best steamed to avoid the leaves becoming waterlogged but in a broth or with noodles, the crinkles trap the flavoursome liquor.

red cabbages Red cabbages mature in winter and, apart from sauerkraut, they are the first choice for pickling, as they stay crisp. Slow-cooked, shredded red cabbage, in alternating layers with red onions and windfall cooking apples, brown sugar and cider vinegar, is a vital part of our Christmas dinner. 'Rouge Tête Noir' can be coaxed to hang on outside in a mild December but otherwise red cabbages often have to be stored.

braised savoy cabbage

This is a wet cabbage recipe with liquor dripping off the crinkly leaves, steam rising up evocatively. Savoy cabbage is also very good as strips in a broth with noodles.

serves 4

1 crinkly-leaved Savoy cabbage
2 garlic cloves
2 tablespoons extra virgin olive oil
2 teaspoons caraway seeds
150ml (5fl oz) white wine or half white wine vinegar and half water
sea salt and black pepper

Destalk the cabbage, wash if necessary and shred into 2.5cm (1in) wide strips. Peel the garlic and slice it very thinly.

In a large pan with a lid, heat the oil to moderately hot and add the garlic and caraway seeds. After a few minutes, tip in the cabbage and stir round evenly to prevent burning, turning down the heat to moderate.

After 3 minutes or so, pour in the liquid, put on the lid and let it reduce. Add some more wine or just water if the liquid has gone before the cabbage is tender enough. Season to taste.

cabbage with juniper berries

Cabbage is a versatile vegetable that presents itself to the kitchen in many forms and can come out again as raw and fierce as coleslaw or soft and comforting as stewed red cabbage. The flavours of your own cabbage cut a few minutes ago compared with a farmer's one cut just yesterday are staggering. You should be delighted with the succulent texture and sweet spiciness of this recipe.

serves 4

100g (3½oz) good butter
1 heaped teaspoon juniper berries, crushed
1 medium cabbage, cored and chopped

Melt the butter gently in a thick-bottomed pan with a tight-fitting lid. Stir in the juniper berries, then add the chopped cabbage and coat in the butter. Put on the lid and shake the pan occasionally to stop the cabbage sticking to the bottom.

After gently cooking for 2 or 3 minutes, take off the lid and check the cabbage. Put the lid back on and repeat until the cabbage is just done a little bit more than *al dente*.

cabbage with juniper berries

VARIETIES

Edible kales come in a wide range of distinctive sizes, shapes, textures and colours. I recommend the following:-

'BORECOLE' and **'DWARF GREEN CURLED'**, which looks like an aerial view of a rainforest.

'RED RUSSIAN', with a wiggly edge and deep purple-red ribs.

'NERO DI TOSCANA', with compact, narrow dark green puckered leaves.

'CARINATA', with intense reddish-purple oval leaves.

kale

Kale plants are probably the most handsome brassicas of all. They are welcome in any stylish ornamental planting scheme, and sea kale, *Crambe maritima*, is one of my favourite plants, with its glaucous pucker-edged leaves under a charming cluster of sweet, honey-scented white flowers.

growing kale

The leaves of kale are tough and heavy-duty, and the plant can stand winter gales and blizzards, as it evolved from life on the cliff-edge in the full blast of ocean storms. This robustness goes hand-in-hand with an eagerness to grow for you: seeds germinate reliably, the plant shoots into growth, and survives very well without any help, just an occasional check for firm anchoring in the soil after storms.

harvesting kale

Kale will provide a reliable supply of leaves all the way through autumn, winter and into the 'winter gap' and emptiness of early spring. These later varieties will even taste better after midwinter frosts. If you are relying on kale for a regular supply of fresh, nutritious winter greens, keep pulling or cutting off the leaves from the bottom up. Many kales will tolerate pulling out the young inner leaves in a 'cut-and-come-again' cycle. These can actually be eaten raw to give salads a substantial leaf. Shredding might make them combine better with other leaves in the salad.

preparing kale

Apart from the tenderest baby leaves, the central rib and the stalks should be separated from the leaf and cooked ahead because they are much tougher. As with spinach, it is easy to rip the leaves off the stalk by pulling them away with one hand, stalk in the other.

steaming kale

The coarser-leaved varieties benefit by being shredded to aid quick cooking and can be steamed or sweated in olive oil in a pan with a lid. Garlic is a good companion to kale cooked young. It might take a surprisingly long time to steam kale until it is tender enough to eat as, unlike soft leaves such as spinach or chard, it doesn't wilt. The tough construction of the leaf surface, to protect against transpiration, also resists the loss of water and collapse of the cells, even after 10 minutes of cooking.

other cooking methods

Tougher, older leaves can be added to stews and soups but might need par-boiling to ensure they are tender at the same time as the other ingredients. You could stew gently in an open pan, though this can concentrate the kale's mineral flavours. To avoid this, simmer cream into it in stages after the kale's moisture has been driven off.

kale tabbouleh

Kale has its apostles: it is undoubtedly
nutritious and available in lean times, but its
toughness and sourness can be a challenge
if you're looking for a substitute for spinach.
Better to recognize its own virtues and play
to its strengths.

serves 4
6 kale leaves
200g (7oz) medium or fine bulgur
   (cracked) wheat
2 super-ripe tomatoes
1 garlic clove, peeled
1 pinch coarse sea salt
4 green peppercorns
1 pinch ground allspice
juice of 1 lemon
1 bunch flat-leaf parsley, roughly chopped
1 shallot, peeled and very finely sliced
1 tablespoon extra virgin olive oil

Cut out and discard the stalks from the kale
leaves and shred the leaves into 5mm (¼in)
strips. Steam the kale for 5 minutes and leave
to stand.

Fine bulgur wheat will absorb enough water
by rinsing it in a sieve, but some coarser
grains need to be simmered for up to
15 minutes to become tender. Follow the
cooking instructions on the packet, then drain.
Cut the tomatoes into tiny chunks and drain
the juice and seeds into a bowl or mortar.

In this bowl grind the garlic with the salt,
peppercorns, allspice and half the lemon juice.
Put this into a serving bowl, along with the kale,
bulgur wheat and chopped tomato, and add
the parsley, shallot and olive oil. Toss all the
ingredients, adding more lemon juice to taste.

kale tabbouleh

kale à la crème

The slightly sour taste and uncompromising
texture of kale is tamed by the comforting
smoothness of the cream. This recipe can also
be baked in the oven, although double cream
works better than single.

serves 4
1 onion
1 carrot
3 garlic cloves
100g (3½fl oz) unsalted butter
3 handfuls kale leaves
sea salt and black pepper
75ml (2½fl oz) single cream
finely grated zest of 1 lemon

Peel and chop the onion. Slice the carrot
into quadrants – lengthways in half and
then lengthways again – and peel and slice
the garlic.

Stew all of these in the butter in a sizeable
pan until soft, adding water if necessary to
prevent the garlic from browning.

Wash the kale and take out and discard the
central rib, shredding the leaves coarsely. Add
the kale to the pan with a pinch of salt and
stir it all around for even cooking. After about
12 minutes of occasional stirring, test the kale
for tenderness.

When it is soft, stir in the cream bit by bit,
finishing with the lemon zest and some salt
and pepper.

roots

jerusalem artichokes

Jerusalem artichokes have a bad reputation for being rampant in the vegetable garden and unsociable in polite company. The small knobbly roots contain the carbohydrate inulin rather than starch or sugar. This is barely digestible, so flatulence is the result. Nonetheless, Jerusalem artichokes are still worth growing and are still worth eating.

growing jerusalem artichokes

The roots throw up a cluster of very tall, vertical stems (up to 3m/10ft tall) with a few small 'sunflower' heads. The vigorous roots help break up clay soils and can survive perfectly well in shady or dry sites, such as under trees or next to walls and hedges.

harvesting and storing jerusalem artichokes

The foliage collapses after a hard frost but the stems can stay there as the tubers taste sweeter after a frost. Spare soil or a mulch can be piled up around them to protect them through very cold weather. The roots can be left in the ground until you want to eat them, unless slug attacks are a problem, or the ground is waterlogged or frozen solid. They are harvested by pulling out the roots. However, if any roots are left in the soil, they are reputed to come up again next year whether they are wanted or not. The tubers store for a week or so if they are not left damp and muddy, or for longer in damp but not wet sand.

preparing jerusalem artichokes

The knobbles on the surface of the tuber make it hard to clean and even harder to peel. Thin-skinned, smooth varieties can be scrubbed with a stiff brush in a bucket of water or easily peeled if big enough. For more knobbly artichokes with thick skins, peeling might be the least trouble, even if you only end up with a little whittled core. A novel technique for cleaning Jerusalem artichokes is to use a clean jet-washer, aiming the jet of clean water, under gentle pressure, at a pile of artichokes.

cooking jerusalem artichokes

Peeled, diced and boiled artichokes can be mashed or puréed but, having no starch, the result will be more watery than mashed potatoes, for example. However, cream of Jerusalem artichoke soup can be one of the world's most sophisticated soups, because a thoroughly sieved purée, totally integrated with the smoothness of cream, takes on an otherworldly texture and subtle taste. Poach artichoke dice with a minced shallot and a bouquet garni in white wine or Noilly Prat, instead of boiling in water. Separate and purée the softened artichokes with the liquor, liquidize and then blend in the cream. A more robust version is to sweat the artichokes with onion or leek, carrot, celery or celeriac and a potato, then simmer in liquid and purée. Jerusalem artichokes roast well, a bit like parsnips, and are a welcome addition to a roast root vegetable collection of celeriac, parsnips, turnips, swede, potatoes and beetroot, with or without garlic and herbs such as rosemary, thyme, bay or sage.

'The roots can be left in the ground until you want to eat them, unless slug attacks are a problem, or the ground is waterlogged or frozen solid.'

Unearth the soil around roots gingerly to avoid damaging them. Use a small garden-fork and start at least 20cm (8in) away from the crown and work your way inwards.

digging roots

Harvesting roots is always exciting. Whatever it is, you've been watching the leafy top growth for months, taking it as a guide for the health and vigour of the roots. Even if you have scrabbled away some soil for a sneak preview of a root or two, you're still not sure how they have done until you dig one up.

lifting and storing potatoes

As a rough guide to potatoes, when there are well-established flowers, the tubers have enough bulk to make them worth eating. To be sure of a substantial size, leave the tubers in the ground for up to two weeks after the tops have died down.

If you have a dry day, the lifted potatoes can be left on top of the ground after any excess soil has been shaken off. This will dry them off a bit, which helps with storage. Double-ply paper potato sacks are ideal for storage in a dry, frost-free covered area.

lifting and storing carrots

Carrots have to reach a fair size, in girth rather than length, to give them enough body to store for any period of time, this can mean more than four months of growth. If they have a woody centre, they will not improve over time but they will lose a noticeable amount of crispness.

Like potatoes, carrots can be stored in paper sacks or in a clamp. They are better being stored with a bit of damp mud on them than still wet from washing. And again, it is better to lift early to avoid excessive slug damage.

lifting and storing other roots

Beetroot, turnips and celeriac all have exposed shoulders that will indicate their size. Their storage needs air to stop wet rot occurring between them, either from wounds or wet mud sticking to them. On the other hand, you don't want them to dry out as losing moisture will toughen and bitter their texture. Keeping

Pull the root slowly out of the ground, gently teasing apart any long, thin rootlets from the neighbours.

them covered on a rack, frost-free indoors works in the medium-term. A box of dampish sharp sand is an alternative form of clamp and can work very well, especially for beetroot.

Parsnips can be stored indefinitely in the ground, providing it is not waterlogged and sluggy. You just dig some up when you need them. The starch in them turns to sugar when they have been frosted and improves the flavour. You can also lift them out of the ground and store them in sand or boxes. It won't matter if the foliage has died back or that you tidy it away.

Wipe off any excess soil from the root. A little bit of damp soil won't hurt but roots should not be stored wet.

girasole niçoise

Jerusalem artichokes in any quantity can have an overpowering flavour, but in such a strongly flavoured sauce they hold their own without offending.

serves 4
1 large onion
½ large fennel bulb (optional)
1 large celery stalk (optional)
100ml (3½fl oz) olive oil
450g (1lb) Jerusalem artichokes
6 large garlic cloves
2 sprigs fresh oregano
2 bay leaves
4 large ripe tomatoes
55g (2oz) stoned black olives, niçoise style
2 tablespoons rinsed and drained capers
1 large bunch fresh parsley
sea salt and black pepper
lemon juice, to taste

Peel the onion and slice it, the fennel and celery coarsely, if using. Stew in the oil in a heavy pan on a moderate heat.

Peel the artichokes, cut into bite-sized chunks and stir them into the pan as they become ready. Smash and peel the garlic, cut into small pieces and add to the pan. Pull the oregano leaves off the stalks and stir them in with the bay leaves. Roughly chop the tomatoes and scrape them into the pan. Stir round and tip in the olives and capers. Finely chop the parsley and stir it in. Test for seasoning.

Simmer steadily, adding a little water to stop the veg from frying, until the artichokes are tender, about 8 minutes.

Serve hot and fresh or let it rest with the lid on until tepid, adding a good squeeze of lemon juice to cut the oiliness.

artichoke crisps

Our neighbour Muriel Hill's Jerusalem artichoke chips are famous. Basically, the artichokes can be treated just the same way as potatoes, peeled, chipped and deep-fried until golden brown. A lighter alternative is offered below.

serves 4 as a snack
1 large garlic clove
sea salt and black pepper
extra virgin olive oil
450g (1lb) Jerusalem artichokes

Smash and peel the garlic and in a mortar, mash it with a good pinch of coarse sea salt, then add 1 tablespoon of the olive oil and continue mixing. Pour on to a shallow dish.

Peel the artichokes one at a time and slice into 5mm (¼in) rounds. Cover and smear the slices in olive oil, adding more oil if necessary to prevent the artichokes discolouring.

Cook the crisps in a hot griddle pan for five minutes, then turn them to cook the other side. Serve sprinkled with salt.

artichoke crisps

VARIETIES

'GLADIATOR' is often recommended as a reliable, general-purpose parsnip for all types of soil.

'TENDER AND TRUE' is vigorous but very well flavoured.

parsnips

Parsnips are the winter vegetable par excellence, benefiting from the cold northern European winters that turn its starches into sugar after hard frosts. The sweet, nutty taste of baked parsnips epitomizes being indoors on a cold winter's day – the sugar in the parsnip lightly caramelized and sticky, the skin glistening, the interior creamy and squashy.

preparing parsnips

The ideal size for a parsnip is over 10cm (4in) long, with the shoulders about the size of a man's thumb. Although the idea of baby parsnips smaller than this sounds nice, they are unlikely to have matured in flavour. If you had to peel parsnips of this size, there would not be much left in the middle, so they probably only need to be scrubbed. Over about 18cm (7in) long, with a shoulder diameter wider than an apple, the parsnip is likely to have a woody centre that will cook more slowly or not satisfactorily at all. This sort of size will have to be peeled. Very large parsnips can be cut into quarters lengthways and any woodiness or wooliness can be seen and cut out.

cooking parsnips

It is not the end of the world if your parsnips are not frosted and therefore not as sweet as they could be. Parsnips have a light fragrant flavour as well as sweetness. When cooking with parsnips, combining with other things, too much sweetness can be overpowering and therefore very limiting in scope. The best parsnip recipes often have the sweetness balanced or negated by other ingredients such as garlic or chilli.

Home-grown parsnips of a modest size are pretty tender and need very little cooking considering their image as a hearty winter root vegetable. They don't need much more than 2 minutes' par-boiling or 5 minutes' boiling or steaming to reach the edge of tenderness. They can then be brushed (or drenched) with olive oil and roasted in an oven, barbecued over charcoal or put under a grill. They can accompany other root vegetables given the same treatment – celeriac, Florence fennel, turnips, coloured beetroot, squash and such-like. If you don't bother with the par-boiling stage, it might be prudent to start the roasting at a reduced heat or at least cover them with a lid or foil so that the cores can get hot before the outsides get burnt. When the roots are almost tender all the way through, turn up the heat or take off the cover to let the edges colour up and caramelize.

roast parsnips in harissa oil

Until you grow and cook your own parsnips, you don't realize how quickly they cook. You can of course just roast the parsnips in plain olive oil: cut in half and roast at 190°C/375°F/Gas 5 covered with foil for 15 minutes, then uncover and roast for a further 5–10 minutes. If roast parsnips don't look very dramatic, they certainly do when cooked in harissa oil. This is the oil that separates from the harissa paste (see page 146). It is bright orange and parsnips stay brightly stained even after cooking.

serves 4
450g (1lb) parsnips
75ml (2½fl oz) harissa oil (see page 146)
sea salt
lime juice (optional)

Preheat the oven to 190°C/375°F/Gas 4.

Top and tail the parsnips and scrub clean. There is no need to peel your own little ones. Cut in halves or quarters according to size – so all the pieces are roughly the same size.

Pour the oil into a large baking tray and warm on top of the stove. Roll the parsnips around in the oil so they are completely covered and orange. Bake in the middle of the preheated oven for about 10–15 minutes, turning as you go. Check for tenderness with a sharp knife, and cover the tray with foil if they are not cooked in the middle. Return to the oven for five minutes or until cooked through.

Serve hot with a sprinkle of salt and maybe a squeeze of lime juice.

roast parsnips in harissa oil

parsnip & chickpea stew

This recipe is just as good made with yellow split peas or lentils, for the same yellow, green and orange effect, optionally flecked with red.

serves 4
1 x 400g (14 oz) can chickpeas, or 100g (3½oz) dried chickpeas, soaked overnight
1 onion, peeled and sliced
2 tablespoons olive oil
1 pinch saffron and/or ½ teaspoon turmeric
2 garlic cloves, peeled and chopped
1 x 2.5cm (1in) piece fresh root ginger, shredded
½ teaspoon cumin seeds (optional)
1 bunch fresh parsley, chopped finely
1 fresh red chilli, deseeded and minced (optional)
225g (8oz) parsnips
1 teaspoon harissa paste (see page 146)
1 bunch fresh coriander, chopped finely
2 handfuls greens (chard, kale, mizuna or spinach)
sea salt and black pepper

For the chickpeas, change the soaking water and bring to a rolling boil, or open the can, drain and rinse. Fry the onion in the oil in a large open pan until softened. Dissolve the saffron or turmeric in 50ml (2fl oz) hot water. Add the garlic, ginger, cumin, if using, chickpeas, saffron or turmeric water, parsley and chilli to the onion and stir, adding extra water to keep it all simmering steadily.

For the parsnips follow the previous recipe, or fry the prepared parsnips in the harissa, until just tender, about 5 minutes, adding the coriander and a little more oil if necessary.

Wash the green leaves, remove the stalks, chop the leaves coarsely and stir them into the chickpeas. When they have wilted, fold in the parsnips. Taste for seasoning.

VARIETIES

ALL-ROUNDERS **'SANTÉ'**, **'PICASSO'** and even **'INTERNATIONAL KIDNEY'**, grown on beyond their **'JERSEY'** new-potato stage.

MASH POTATOES **'SAXON'**, **'BRITISH QUEEN'** or **'WILJA'**.

BAKED, CHIPS AND ROAST POTATOES **'ESTIMA'**, **'DÉSIRÉE'**, **'KING EDWARD'** and **'MARIS PIPER'**.

main-crop potatoes

These are the spuds of traditional British cooking, nearly as much a staple as bread, but now waning in popularity. In the past, allotment holders and gardeners with big vegetable patches expected to grow a year's supply of potatoes themselves. The growing season for all potatoes is short so the emphasis was always on growing big ones that would store well until next year's crop. It was all about getting in a big crop, not pleasing epicurean tastes.

Nowadays, gardeners would question the economics of growing all their own spuds since they are relatively cheap to buy and take up a lot of growing space. Even if it was worthwhile, who would want to rely on using Lindane dust against eelworm, Metaldehyde against slugs and Bordeaux mixture against blight, and still eat the spuds nearly every meal any more?

growing main-crop potatoes

If you do need to go for quantity, but organically because bought potatoes will still have a comparable toxic taint, there are modern potato varieties that resist pests and diseases in the first place, such as the all-rounders listed above.

Growing small quantities of each variety you choose leaves you less vulnerable to catastrophic failure; you are spreading the risk, even if you win some and you lose some. You have greater freedom of choice, you can work backwards from what kind of spuds you like and how you prefer to cook them.

mashed potatoes

Mashed potatoes need dry, floury types (see above). Obviously a big size makes peeling easier. If spuds are diced too small, they have oozed a starchy soup by the time they are tender enough for hand-mashing. Apparently, proteins are necessary to hold the texture smooth, so butter or fatty milk should go in before the mashing begins.

baked jacket potatoes

Baked jacket potatoes can use floury ones to absorb an indulgent topping. Firmer ones like 'Estima' or 'Désirée' will be less saturated. Salt and olive oil can be rubbed on the skin to help crisp it up.

chips

If you want chips to be crisp outside but fluffy inside, don't go straight for a floury potato as it will go soggy from absorbing so much fat. 'King Edward' and 'Maris Piper' will resist until the last minute.

roast and sautéed potatoes

Roast potatoes cook for longer than chips so even 'King Edward' potatoes will be crisp and brown all over. Just as for sautéed potatoes, soft crumbs of well-cooked potato on the outer surfaces will absorb the cooking fat and go brown. By par-boiling first, then lightly sautéing chunks (instead of slices), potatoes can be roasted successfully without a joint of meat beside them and in much less time.

leek & potato soup

Main-crop potatoes are almost a different vegetable to young baby ones, especially floury types that are so good baked, roasted or mashed. Floury also means starchy, and this helps to thicken soups and sauces. It also gives *potage bonne femme* if liquidized or blended.

serves 4
2 large leeks
85g (3oz) unsalted butter
4 large floury potatoes
sea salt and black pepper

Trim and clean the leeks and chop into 3mm (⅛in) rounds. Stew the leeks in the butter in a large pan with a lid on to prevent frying.

Peel the potatoes and dice into 1cm (½in) cubes. Tip them into the leek and stir thoroughly. Add a pinch of salt and pepper, cover with water and bring to a simmer. Stir occasionally, simmering until the potato is very soft, about 15 minutes.

Dish up chunky, or liquidize for smoothness.

dauphinoise potatoes

This is a classic French recipe (although many add some Gruyère cheese to the layers). The Italian version is even easier for hob-cooking. Just substitute full-cream milk for the cream and butter; then simmer the layers of potato and garlic under a cover of milk until tender. Waxy old potatoes are essential for this as they have a stability that can take slow cooking.

serves 4–6
4 large waxy potatoes
1 large garlic clove
25g (1oz) unsalted butter
sea salt
300ml (10fl oz) double cream

Preheat the oven to 180°C/350°F/Gas 4.

Peel the potatoes, cut them in half and then cut into 3mm (⅛in) slices. Peel the garlic and slice paper-thin.

Butter an ovenproof baking dish and lay on the first layer of potato slices.

Drop on a few little knobs of butter and strew on some garlic flakes and a tiny pinch of salt. Spread on a small smear of cream. Carry on building up the layers, but don't worry that you will run out of garlic and butter.

Finish with a layer of cream.

Bake for 30 minutes in the preheated oven.

dauphinoise potatoes

swede

Swede is another member of the extensive Brassica family, and is typically vigorous and hardy. It seems to have a coarse and robust personality, but the cooked flesh is surprisingly demure. It is very much a winter vegetable, tasting sweeter after frost, and the fleshy root is best eaten when it is mature: there is nothing to be gained by eating it tiny and young.

growing swede

The growing season can range from four to eight months, and deciding when to sow it and where to sow it takes some forethought. It will occupy a settled site, taking about 30cm (1ft) for each plant, but the space will be cleared when you dig it up.

Traditionally, gardeners would sow the seeds over the summer in anticipation of a hard winter, and harvest them from autumn into winter, and even into early spring. As long as it can be retrieved from the ground, swede is a very valuable source of food in the middle of winter either for man or beast. You can leave swedes in the ground until you need them and only dig them out if you are afraid of being frozen out for a long spell. However, varieties of swede left in the ground for a very long time stop growing in size and seem to increase in density, with an inedible woody core in the centre.

preparing swede

Swede skin is tough and thick and peeling seems to reveal two layers to it. The peel should go through the pale inner layer down to the flesh underneath. Swede flesh is pale yellow and goes a pretty apricot-orange on cooking.

eating and cooking swede

If you grow your own and dig it out just when you need it, the flavour and texture will be far better than any bought swede. If a farmer digs up a swede, it will join a pile already harvested efficiently by machine and its hard skin lets him get away with plonking it in crates a ton at a time, and basically people will be eating cattle food.

Crops can be few and far between in March, and the new flush of young swede leaves can be used as spring greens and cooked like cabbage. (Old over-wintered leaves might suffer from rot, powdery mildew and chew-holes.) Swede flesh steams well and 2.5cm (1in) chunks take about 7–10 minutes to reach tenderness. For mashed recipes, it boils in water for 15 minutes. Swede can be substituted for other root vegetables such as celeriac or turnips, and its mildness allows it to absorb flavourings from garlic, herbs and spices. The sugar in it fries nicely in oil, and its delicate flavour goes well with plain butter.

swede french-style

Swede has a gentle flavour and comforting texture that belies its stuck-in-a-field, cattle-food status. Lightly boiled and dressed with a little really good butter, it can be a delicious treat. This recipe gives it a French twist.

serves 4
1 medium swede
1 garlic clove, peeled
1 small bunch fresh parsley, chopped
about 55g (2oz) butter, softened

Peel all the skin from the swede through to orange flesh. Cut the flesh into one-bite chunks and steam until tender.

Crush the peeled garlic in a mortar and grind in the chopped parsley. Mix into the butter.

Check the swede for softness with the point of a sharp knife. Toss the hot swede with the garlic and parsley butter, and let it melt over.

mashed swede & carrot

This is another mainstay of our Christmas dinner, and is equally anticipated as an ingredient of bubble and squeak on Boxing Day.

serves 4–6
1 medium swede
4 carrots
sea salt and black pepper
55g (2oz) unsalted butter

Peel the swede and cut into 1cm (½in) cubes. Put it into a pan of fast-boiling, salted water.

Top and tail the carrots and scrub out any soily cracks. Chop the carrots into 1cm/½in slices and drop into the water with the swede.

When they are both soft, after about 10 minutes, drain away all the cooking water. Mash them with a potato masher or in a processer, but leave some texture.

Stir in the butter, and liberally sprinkle with black pepper.

swede french-style

alliums
leeks

The grow-your-own gardener is not likely to be harbouring dreams of finding fame as a prize-leek grower. Growing leeks as big as is humanly possible and showing them off around the country has got nothing to do with growing something delicious to eat. Young leeks, all fresh and green, are an altogether more sensual pleasure.

Leeks have always been popular because they can usually stand outside, ready and fresh all winter. Onions on the other hand have to be stored indoors. Leeks can have a long growing season so they are quite likely to get big and substantial in height and girth. The leaves will be all the worse for wear, having been out in all weathers, and will droop forlornly.

A winter leek will get a lot of its leaves cut off in the kitchen but this is just the time of year that anything green is at a premium. Tall-growing varieties will have a higher proportion of green in their core than short fat ones. However, the exact variety, and more especially how deep they are planted, will have more bearing.

cooking leeks
Where recipes call for leek to be chopped up among other ingredients, it is more economical to have short white leeks such as 'Carentan' or 'Musselburgh'.

Sometimes it is nice to have some green colour in recipes featuring leeks in winter so colourful relations of 'Musselburgh', just as hardy, are 'Bleu de Solaise' and 'Tadorna'.

Leeks that are presented in the dish, like baked or braised leeks, leeks baked in cream or in a gratin, are better selected from narrow leeks, but it is not really that critical. Among any collection of growing leeks, there will always be some that seem skinnier and dishes can be made according to what is to hand. Dishes can be delayed, waiting for the right vegetable to become ready – the expectation usually improves the enjoyment.

baby leeks
Baby leeks can be pulled after a couple of months' growing. They have built up a number of rings inside and have begun to stand rigid. Quick-growing varieties are best for this, like 'Swiss Giant – Evita' and 'Electra'. Because they never last long enough to grow big and thick, it doesn't matter if they have been planted thickly and become congested. They can be thinned rather than cleared from one end. They can even be grown in containers like this.

barbecued leeks

When the leeks are about a little finger's width, you can start eating them. Cleaning is no big deal: cut off the bottom where the fibrous white roots join the stem. Check there is no yellowish pad still on the stem. Cut down to where the green leaves are clean and undamaged. Peel off a layer if there is surface damage. Starting a few inches up from the bottom, cut a long slit up to the top from one of the sides to the centre. Winkle out any soil underwater or under a running tap.

per person
2–4 young leeks, depending on size
1 tablespoon olive oil or melted butter
dressing of choice (see page 220)

Blanch the leeks in boiling water for 5 minutes and drain well. Paint the leeks individually with olive oil or melted butter.

Lay them together on a rack or grill or ribbed griddle pan and cook for 8–12 minutes, turning them as necessary.

Serve with a dressing, commensurate with the trouble you have just taken – it's worth it.

baked leeks

Leeks somehow manage to be mild and all-pervading at the same time. They smell delicious cooking in butter, but it can be a bit too much sometimes. While massively endowed leeks are economic to cook, much smaller, younger ones are much more fun.

serves 4
2 or 3 medium leeks
55g (2oz) unsalted butter
1 small carton single cream
1 small carton soured cream
sea salt and black pepper
paprika, to taste (optional)

Preheat the oven to 180°C/350°F/Gas 4.

Clean the leeks and cut diagonally into 15mm (⅝in) rings.

Gently melt the butter in a heavy pan with a tight-fitting lid. Mix in the leeks, cover and let them steam away strongly, but not fry. Turn the leeks out into an ovenproof dish after 10 minutes.

Mix the two creams together and drown the leek rings, adding salt and pepper to taste.

Bake in the preheated oven, at moderate so as not to separate the cream, for 25 minutes.

Sprinkle with paprika, if desired.

baked leeks

leaves & herbs

hardy herbs

Before the concept of global warming entered the public consciousness, many gardeners wouldn't have considered winter a time for green leaves. But nowadays we don't have to rely on kale, chard and beet for all our fresh green vitamins.

leaves   Surprising as it may seem to someone who has never grown it, **LETTUCE** can be just as much a winter salad crop as a summer one. It can sit parked on well-drained soil all through the winter in any southern or well-sheltered garden. It won't overgrow itself, nor will it bolt and run to seed. So one plant will be available for light cropping for months. You might need several plants to give enough for a bowlful, but the leaves will be surprisingly good.

Members of the **ROCKET AND MUSTARD** family are just as hardy, and plants established in early autumn will keep going right through into spring. Picking over a few plants will reveal enough small tender leaves for one eating.

Baby **PAK-CHOI** might survive planting out as early as February and individual leaves can be plucked off for raw eating in a mixed salad. They have a lovely bluish bloom and striking indented leaves. '**MÂCHE**' or corn salad or lamb's lettuce will perk up surprisingly early in the year and its sweetness will mollify a salad of excessively hot rocket or mustard. A little bunch will grow from a central point just above the ground yet somehow manages to attract quite a bit of grit in among its leaves. If you can suspend it in enough water to float it, the grit falls out and you can scoop out the leaves rather than tip them out through a colander. **MIZUNA** will over-winter usually and small, tender leaves can be picked out from the centre once a week or so. A small winter leaf will be nicer to eat than an overgrown one in spring or summer.

herbs   There are some reliable herbs that can be picked all through the winter. They might not have the intensity of flavour that they might from months of sunbathing in the summer but what they do have will be life-affirming and welcome. **THYME**, and its many variants, like lemon thyme, will hug the ground and shrink from their former glory, but it will still yield enough single leaves for plenty of flavour. **SAGE** will retain enough leaves for harvesting, especially if there are a flush of new leaves that came after a light shearing in the summer. Even dry and curled leaves will wake up in the cooking. **ROSEMARY** will stand the winter as its needle leaves are designed to ignore both hot and cold weather. It is better to harvest a few tips rather than snap off whole branches: the rule for winter harvesting is 'lightly does it'; it's better to appreciate what you are lucky enough to gather not take it all for granted.

BAY benefits from being an evergreen tree or shrub, and this will give it the resilience to see it through all weathers. If you pick off individual leaves or small sprigs, choose exposed ones from the south side of the plant, as they will have enjoyed whatever weak winter sunshine there was.

garlic & herb oil

If you are lucky enough to have a bay tree or rosemary bush, they will keep going through winter, giving an endless supply of exciting flavours. They are much more robust than the ephemeral summer herbs, and they suit winter cooking better.

makes 450ml (16fl oz)
450ml (16fl oz) extra virgin olive oil
3 sprigs fresh rosemary
6 bay leaves
1 garlic bulb

Preheat the oven to 120°C/250°F/Gas ½.

In an ovenproof bowl, pour in the oil and add the herbs.

Trim off the old stalks and any roots from the garlic. Cut the whole bulb of garlic horizontally, right across the middle. Drop it in the bowl and let the whole thing stew in the very low oven for a few hours. Don't let the garlic deep-fry in the oil because it will go very bitter, although the oil will still be good.

After gentle stewing the garlic pulp can be squeezed out and used in other recipes – it's very useful in a full-on sort of way. The oil is full of herb flavour and can be used as a shortcut in cooking – no need for garlic or herbs – or for balancing flavours precisely.

bouquet garni

If you have any of the following herbs – parsley, tarragon, chervil, oregano, sage or bay leaves – you can make a bouquet garni to flavour dishes such as soups, stews and stocks. Traditionally the herbs would be left with long stalks and one or two of each would be bundled together and tied up with a leek leaf wrapped round and pinned with something like a tooth-pick. The bundle would be retrieved before serving the dish.

makes one 450g (1lb) jam-jarful
2 sprigs parsley
3 sprigs tarragon
2 sprigs oregano
1 sprig sage
3 bay leaves
2 sprigs thyme
1 pinch green or black peppercorns
300ml (⅔ pint) oil or white wine

Remove the leaves from the parsley, tarragon, oregano, sage and thyme stalks and chop finely using a rocking hachoir. To these add the bay leaves and the oil or wine. Mix these all together in a jam jar, shaking to exclude any air from the herbs.

Alternatively, put the herb mixture omitting the bay leaves and the liquid, into resealable plastic pouches and freeze if you can get them frozen very quickly. You can crumble the herbs while they are still frozen in the bags.

dressings & sauces

SALAD DRESSINGS

Sometimes the freshest young vegetables have an innocence of taste that would be overwhelmed, if not sullied, by any kind of dressing. Only after the novelty of a new season's crop has worn off will dressings serve to bring out the flavours.

serves 2
lemon dressing
1 tablespoon extra virgin olive oil
½ tablespoon freshly squeezed lemon juice
1 pinch sea salt

balsamic and mustard dressing
3 glugs extra virgin olive oil
1 glug balsamic vinegar
1 teaspoon wholegrain mustard
½ teaspoon caster sugar
1 pinch sea salt
white wine vinegar, to taste

pomegranate dressing
2 glugs extra virgin olive oil
1 teaspoon pomegranate syrup
1 small pinch sea salt
2 twists black pepper
3 tablespoons cold water
lemon juice, to taste

Stir all the ingredients together and rest before serving to allow the flavours to infuse.

garlic dressing

1 garlic clove, peeled
2 pinches sea salt
2 glugs olive oil
2 tablespoons lemon juice

Pound the garlic into a mush with the salt. Add the oil, stirring all the while and work into an emulsion. Stir in the lemon juice.

SALAD SAUCES

sauce hollandaise
Sauce Hollandaise is a smooth buttery, lemony emulsion that brings out the flavour of asparagus or broccoli very well. It should be made and then eaten in a warm and gentle manner.

serves 2
2 tablespoons white wine
3 black peppercorns, bruised
3 medium egg yolks, beaten
3 tablespoons cold water
125g (4½oz) best butter, softened
1 squeeze of lemon juice
sea salt

Put the wine and peppercorns in a small pan and boil to reduce by half. Take out the peppercorns. Add the egg yolks to the reduced wine and whisk over a medium-hot pan of water, adding 1 tablespoon of the cold water to the mixture as you go. Add the softened butter, a small knob at a time, while whisking. Add the remaining cold water, a squeeze of lemon juice and test for salt.

sauce maltaise
To the basic Hollandaise, add the juice of a small orange (a blood-orange classically), although a lime is more apposite sometimes, and some finely grated zest or thinly cut peel.

index

acknowledgements

Special thanks to those who have
contributed to this book.

Thanks to Carol and Neil Klein for
their time, passion and energy.

All photography by Howard Sooley,
except page 163 (RHS Collection).